A PARSON'S HOLIDAY

A PARSON'S HOLIDAY

BEING AN ACCOUNT OF A TOUR IN INDIA, BURMA, AND CEYLON, IN THE WINTER OF 1882-83

ALLEN WILLIAM OSBORNE BIRD

GYAN

Published by

Gyan Publishing House
5, Ansari Road
Daryaganj, New Delhi-110002
Phone: 011-47034999, 9811692060
E-mail: books@gyanbooks.com

Distribution Network
gyanbooks.com
India, USA, Canada, UK, Australia

ISBN: 978-93-7133-095-4 (PB)

First Published, 1885

2nd Impression 2025

Printed at: Gyan Press, Delhi.

A PARSON'S HOLIDAY

Author: ALLEN WILLIAM OSBORNE BIRD

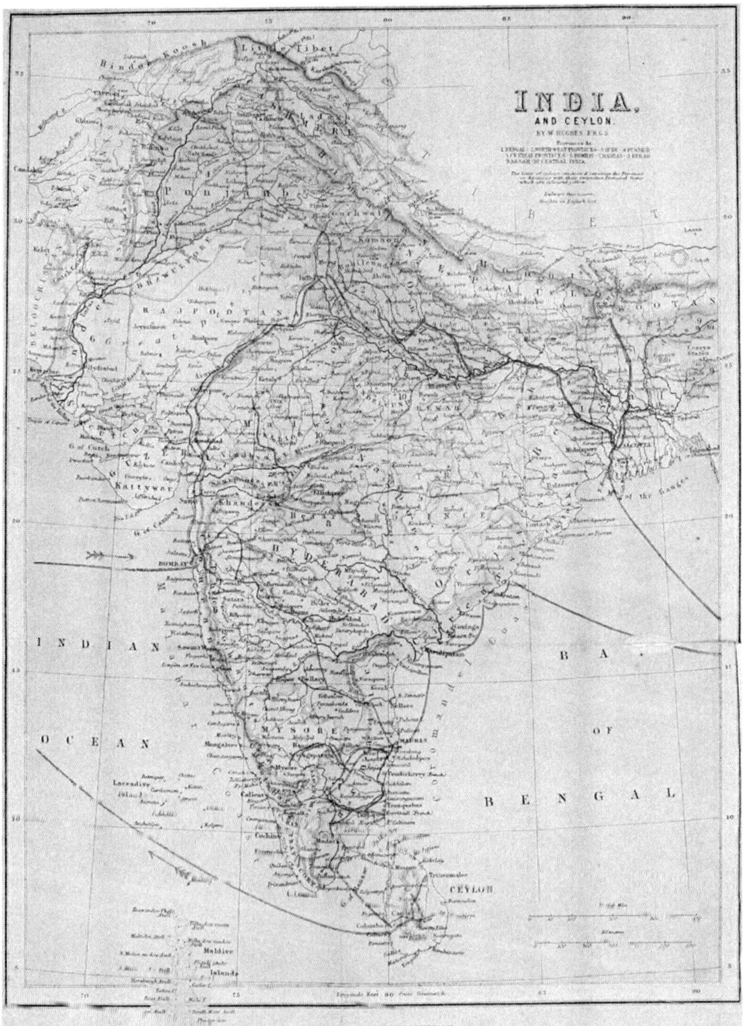
INDIA,
AND CEYLON.
BY W. HUGHES F.R.G.S.
INDIAN
OCEAN
BAY
OF
BENGAL
CEYLON
BOMBAY
MADRAS
MYSORE
HYDERABAD
Punjaub
Kattywar
Maldive
Islands
Laccadive
Little Tibet
GEORGE PHILIP & SON, LONDON & LIVERPOOL.

A PARSON'S HOLIDAY;

BEING AN ACCOUNT OF A

TOUR IN INDIA, BURMA, AND CEYLON,

IN THE

WINTER OF 1882–83.

BY

W. OSBORN B. ALLEN,

VICAR OF SHIRBURN, OXON.

TENBY:

F. B. MASON, PRINTER, "OBSERVER" OFFICE.

1885.

TO THE

MEMORY OF MY FATHER,

FORMERLY MEMBER OF THE LEGISLATIVE COUNCIL IN INDIA,

WHO SPENT HIS LIFE IN DOING GOOD BOTH TO

ENGLISHMEN AND NATIVES,

AT HOME AND ABROAD;

AND TO THE

MEMORY OF MY MOTHER,

WHO WAS HIS WORTHY AND BELOVED HELPMATE,

THIS BOOK

IS DEDICATED.

PREFACE.

FAMILY circumstances have delayed the publication of this little book, and it is now more than two years since I made the tour herein described. Yet India changes (in some respects) so slowly, that I venture to think that the delay has not robbed the book of all interest, nor made the whole work out of date.

I feel that an apology is necessary for adding to the numerous works which have been already written by the chance travellers who have wintered in India. My defence is that, although these works have been full of varied interest, yet none of them have treated the subject quite from my standpoint. The Parson who travels looks at things with a professional eye, and the observations he makes have an interest of their own, especially for his brother-Clergymen.

A greater apology is necessary to those Indian officials, or residents, or missionaries, who may look into this little work. I will beg them to remember that I cannot hope to have escaped all errors, and that I have probably uttered many crude and ill-considered remarks. They will have patience with one who does not set up for a critic of their life-long labours, and who is aware that he has but skimmed the surface of subjects about which they are past-masters of knowledge.

Concerning the vexed question of the proper spelling

of Indian names I have neither tried to be consistent nor over scrupulous. It would be pedantry in me to affect a spelling, which is often unfamiliar to English readers, and which, though nearer no doubt to the Oriental sound, yet would only puzzle those who have no knowledge of Indian pronunciation and nomenclature. I have therefore been content to write "Poona" rather than "Puna," "Lucknow" rather than "Lakhnau," and "Delhi" rather than "Dîhli." In nearly all instances I have followed the authority of the distinguished Mr. W. W. Hunter, whose *Indian Empire* is a store-house of facts and learning. But I fear I have not always been guided by him, nor always been consistent with myself.

Other books of reference to which I am indebted are Fergusson's *Handbook of Architecture*, Rhys David's *Buddhism*, Oldenberg's *Life of Buddha*, *The Burman* by Shway Yoe, *Hinduism* by Monier Williams, Sir E. Tennent's *Ceylon*, and the *Handbook to Agra and Lucknow* compiled by H. G. Keene, besides various Missionary Reports giving statistics of their several Stations.

I cannot here attempt to express my thanks to each of those kind hosts and friends, who made my holiday so enjoyable. I will only say to them all that I can never be sufficiently grateful for the constant kindness and unselfish attention which they bestowed on me and my concerns.

SHIRBURN, OXON,
April, 1885.

CONTENTS.

CHAPTER I. PAGE.

Introduction, Voyage, Bombay, Towers of Silence, Caves of Elephanta, Poona, Temple of Parvathi, Leprous Hospital, Missionaries, Cowley Fathers, Education, Schools, Breaking-up Day at High School 1–22

CHAPTER II.

Karli Cave, Railway Travelling, Station Life, Baroda, Rajputana, The Clans, Ajmere, Mayo College, The Eurasians, Jeypore, Maharajah's Palace, Ambir, Feudatory States 23–41

CHAPTER III.

Delhi, History of the Mogul Empire, Mohammedans in India, Palace, Jumma Musjid, Kutub Minar, Cambridge Mission, S. Stephen's College, Agra, Palace, Tombs, Taj Mahal, Futtehpore Sikri, Sekundra .. 42–62

CHAPTER IV.

Cawnpore, The Mutiny, The Massacre, Memorial Well, Lucknow, History of Oudh, Imambara, Residency, Viceroy's Camp, Durbar, Martinière College, Government of India, Indian Civil Service 63–83

CHAPTER V.

Benares, Illumination of Ghâts, Idolatry, Manufactures, Journey to Calcutta, Darjeeling, The Himalayas, Tibetan Lamaism, Calcutta, Government House, Buildings, Gardens, Oxford Mission 84–104

CHAPTER VI.

History of Burma, Rangoon, The Burmese, Buddhism, History and Doctrines of Gautama, Pagodas, Statues, Kioungs, Monks, Offerings, Christianity and Buddhism compared 105–126

CHAPTER VII.

Missionaries in Burma, Dr. Marks, Christmas Day at Rangoon, Prome, Independent Burma, Nga-pee, Moulmein, Caves, Timber Yards, Elephants, Pegu, A Difficult Journey, Voyage from Rangoon to Madras, Salt Tax 127–147

CHAPTER VIII.

Madras, Tamils, Native Christians, Bangalore, Native Clergymen, Mysore, Seringapatam, Tipu Saib, Tomb of Hyder Ali, The Deserted Bungalow, Caste Rules, Tanjore, Temples of Southern India, Schwartz, Decayed Royalty 148–167

CHAPTER IX.

Trichinopoly, Srirangham, Mission Work, Schools, An Evening Meeting, Madura, Trimul Naik, The Church Establishment, Tinnevelly, History of its Missions, The Effect of the Famine, Statistics .. 168–185

CHAPTER X.

Tinnevelly, Palamcottah, A Drive in a "Bandy," Nazareth, Sunday in a Native Christian Village, Mission Life, Orphanages, Evangelistic Work, Life of a Missionary, Sir R. Temple on Missions, Mudalûr, Mengnanapuram, A Self-denying Life, "Society Bishops," Tuticorin, Leave India 186–207

CHAPTER XI.

Colombo, Inhabitants of Ceylon, Kandy, Failure of Coffee Shrub, Tooth Temple, Anaradhapura, Dagobas, Ruins, Sacred Bo Tree, Proposed Annexation to India, Oil Factory, Homeward Voyage, Egypt, Cairo, Ismailya, Block in the Canal, Discoverer of Pithom, Return to England 208–225

A PARSON'S HOLIDAY.

I HAD long had a wish to visit India, and in the autumn of last year (1882) it seemed possible to accomplish my purpose. And thus on the evening of October 4th I found myself in the night train for Dover, hurrying away from London, and intending to be absent from England for a six months' holiday. During these six months I travelled through India, Burma and Ceylon, and though I did not leave the ordinary beaten tracks, yet I think my experiences may interest others. I know that India has become a winter touring ground, that numbers of travellers pass through it every cool season, and that the T. G. (or travelling gent.) is becoming a common object in every large railway station. I know also that numerous books of travels, expressing more or less superficial opinions, and more or less inaccurate descriptions of people and places, have been already published. I may therefore be asked why I should think it necessary to publish another work, which will probably possess all the faults of its predecessors without any countervailing merits of its own. To this I would answer that in spite of all that has been written on the subject there is still a great ignorance amongst English people of things Indian. The Indian official is too busy to care to take the trouble to put his experiences on record. He has also lived so long amongst Oriental sights and customs, and these things have become so familiar to himself, that he thinks they are equally well known by his countrymen at home. Added to this, he usually spends his life in one part of the country, and never has time or desire to see anything of other parts of India. If he cared to do so, he could enlighten most of us about a hundred matters of which we are densely ignorant, and yet which make up the life of two hundred millions of our fellow subjects. But as a rule he maintains silence, and only wonders at the little knowledge possessed, and the quaint mistakes made, by his stay-at-home brother. It therefore seems to fall to the lot of the chance traveller to put on record his crude impressions in the hope that what he says may induce more of his countrymen to take an interest in England's greatest dependency, and if possible to see with their own eyes the wonders of the East. The politician and the professor, the sportsman and the travelling lady, have already given their experiences of a tour in India to the world. It remains for the parson to add his quota to the general farrago. He cannot hope to have done more than skimmed the surface of the many difficult questions which are constantly arising in India. He knows that his knowledge is very superficial, his opinions very hastily formed, his ideas very crude and undigested. But things that may have been omitted by other writers have perhaps struck him, and aspects of social life and missionary effort, and problems of Church government and educational progress, which other writers overlooked, interested him. He therefore ventures to think that these hasty notes of a winter tour may be not without use even to those who are most experienced in Indian matters. While to those who are less learned in Eastern places and customs, he hopes they may prove somewhat interesting.

Therefore without further preface or apology I would begin to describe my holiday tour. I need not linger long over the voyage. The Overland Route has been so often described, that it is difficult to find anything fresh to relate about that. From Calais to Brindisi there was a dusty, tiresome, railway journey, only broken for me at Ancona, where I tried in vain to get on board the P. and O. steamer. It may be as well to warn intending travellers that it is very rarely that these steamers touch at Ancona. The harbour is small and badly lighted, and therefore although their contract compels them to touch there "weather permitting," yet this clause often affords them an excuse for not doing so. It is better therefore either to join the steamer at Venice, or at Brindisi. I spent a night sitting on the pier at Ancona with a number of Italian sailors, who apparently did without sleep, and passed the time in chaffing each other and laughing at me for expecting any steamer to pick me up. In the morning I was able to go on by train to Brindisi, where on Sunday evening, October 8th, I went on board the steamer which was to carry me to Bombay. From Brindisi to Alexandria we had several Egyptian refugees and distinguished officials as our fellow passengers. They were hastening back, now that Egypt was once more quiet, and were full of anecdotes of narrow escapes incurred during the days of massacre before the bombardment. On the 12th we sighted the lighthouse at Alexandria, and as we steamed into the harbour everyone was on the look out to see the damage done to the Forts by the bombardment. Ours was the first steamer which had touched at Alexandria, since the beginning of the revolt, and everyone was anxious to land to see the destruction which had been caused by the great fire. The large "Place" in the centre of the European quarter was an utter ruin, the whole of it having been entirely burnt; but other parts of the city seemed very little injured. The British soldier was in occupation everywhere, making himself thoroughly at home. He apparently made himself understood by talking English in a loud tone of voice, and a free use of signs. We heard one bargaining with a native female fruit seller, and because he did not like what he got, he shouted at her, "Look here; I say; not good." And she apparently understood him. From Alexandria our steamer went round to Port Said, and through the Suez Canal, as the railway through Egypt was not yet in working order. The voyage down the Red Sea was the hottest part of my experiences, the thermometer standing one day at 96°. We landed at Aden, and saw the Crater Camp and the Tanks, and wondered at the cindery appearance and strong fortifications of this rocky corner of Arabia. We had lovely weather in the Indian Ocean, and passed the days in quiet idleness, reclining in long deck chairs, playing chess, discussing our fellow passengers, and watching the ordinary boardship flirtations. It was a quiet, pleasant time, which seemed to rest everyone, and will be long remembered. But each day the ship's run was anxiously noted, and at last we were in sight of Bombay harbour. Now it seemed that one's real journeying was to begin, and one was really to see the land of which one had heard so much. The landing at the Apollo Bunder was accomplished with a certain amount of trouble, but when my packages were collected, I was soon driven through the crowded streets of Bombay to the Byculla Hotel. There the landlord was a Parsee, the bedroom servants Hindus, and the waiters Mahommedans; there were mosquito curtains on the bed, and verandahs all round the house; punkahs were being pulled, and the smell of sandal wood, mingled with strange cries, came up from the bazaar; a jackal howled in the distance, and I tried to say a sentence in Hindustani; and then I really felt that at last I was in India. That first night, when I was alone, with all its fresh new feelings, stands out distinct and memorable. But in the morning there were many new, strange incidents, which kept one's eyes and ears fully employed. There was first the look of the streets; the throng of natives was very surprising. One did not at first distinguish the different castes; that experience came later. But the mere mass and crowd of dark-skinned, white-robed, turbaned natives filling the streets, riding on the tramcars, and sitting at the shop doors, showed one how populous the city is. The public buildings are very fine; and the principal streets are broad and well paved. In the native quarter I got my first sight of a bazaar, and began to learn the different native industries and trades. Besides enjoying the sights of the streets, I was shown the Towers of Silence, which are the Parsees' burial places, and are so well described in Professor Monier Williams's *Modern India*. We drove to the foot of a hill, and then followed a footpath which led us to a gateway. On ringing at the gate, and showing our order, we were admitted into a large walled enclosure, which seemed to cover the whole summit of the hill, and to be several acres in extent. The views over the harbour and town were very extensive and beautiful, and this is one of the prettiest sites in Bombay. The enclosure was laid out with paths and flowering shrubs, and in it there were some groves of tall trees. The place seemed very still and quiet, and at first we saw no signs of any burial place. But soon our guide pointed out to us three low towers, which appeared to be about 40 feet high, and about 60 feet in diameter. Round the top of these towers, and on the surrounding trees, there sat quantities of vultures, which were waiting to devour the corpses, which are placed inside the towers. We were not allowed to approach nearer than about 50 yards to the towers, but we were shown a model of a tower in the guide's house, and from that and his descriptions we learned the manner of the Parsee funeral. The friends of the deceased bring the body to the enclosure between the hours of four and six in the evening, and there leave it in the hands of certain members of their religion, who are specially deputed to perform the funeral rites. These caretakers of the dead are the only persons permitted to enter the towers, and have sole charge of the bodies, after they have been brought to the enclosure. At sunset, when no one else is near, the bodies are placed by these officials inside the towers, each one on a separate bier, and there left. No sooner is the door of the tower shut, than the vultures swoop down, and devour the corpses there placed for their delectation. In the morning the officials again enter the tower, and collect any bones or scraps of clothing that may be left, and these are, I believe, consumed by fire. There is an arrangement made for the drainage of the interior of the tower, and the whole place is kept beautifully clean and neat. The great object of this mode of disposal of the dead is to resolve the corpse as quickly as possible into its component elements, and return these to the earth from whence they were taken. It may sound disgusting to a Western mind, but a Parsee would consider our mode of leaving the corpse to be slowly destroyed by natural corruption a much more unhealthy and disgusting method, and he would argue that the swoop of the heaven-sent birds is a much less horrible mode of destroying the empty casket of the soul than leaving it to the slower process of the worm and the pit. Certainly in the Towers of Silence, as seen by the casual visitor or the sorrowing survivor, there is nothing to shock the most sensitive spirit, and every praise must be given to the Parsee community for the care they take of the enclosure and its buildings.

Besides seeing the Towers of Silence, we also visited the Caves of Elephanta. These are situated on an island in the harbour, some six miles from the Apollo Bunder. We hired a steam launch to take us to the place. We landed at a pier built of large stones, and walked for some hundreds of yards up a steep rocky staircase, which led to the caves. We were surrounded by a number of the male inhabitants of the island, who desired to sell us curiosities, such as coloured beetles, butterflies, bright red seeds, nests, &c. They were a dark coloured race, of a lower type than the Bombay native, and very possibly belonged to an earlier aboriginal people. The caves themselves were cut in the perpendicular face of a rocky hill, overlooking the landing place. The great temple is 133 feet broad, 130 feet long, and 20 feet high; the roof is supported by massive pillars, with ornamental capitals, which are all cut out of the living rock. There is a colossal bust with three heads, opposite the entrance, supposed to represent the Hindu Trinity. There are also several other gigantic figures, but all are much mutilated. Besides the great temple there are some smaller caves and shrines. At one of these, one of the native inhabitants of the island pulled off his turban and worshipped. He did it quite quietly and unobtrusively, and without any wish to attract attention. It showed that these old-world temples were still used by these primitive islanders. The idol which he worshipped was the "linga," which is the symbol of the creative principle or reproductive power in nature throughout India, and though possibly it was originally chosen by philosophers as the best expression of the great First Cause, yet the less educated worshippers have made it an excuse for immorality, and have turned what might have been originally a high conception of the Creator into a sanction for impure and corrupt rites. The Caves of Elephanta are not of great antiquity, and probably were excavated about 1000 A.D.

From Bombay I went by the G. I. P. railway to Poona. The distance is 119 miles, and the time taken on the journey is about six hours, but during that time one rises about 2000 feet, and gets the most beautiful views over the country. For after running through a rich flat land for 60 miles, the train begins to ascend the Bhore Ghâts, up very steep gradients. The line is magnificently engineered, and the views as the train climbs the hills are grand in the extreme. The rocks glowed red in the light of the setting sun, and the precipices rose nearly perpendicularly, and there were thin waterfalls, which fell and seemed to get lost before they touched the ground. These Ghâts run like a wall all down the west coast of India, and when they are surmounted, one reaches a great tableland, which extends nearly to Madras. So steep is this wall of rock, that the Krishna and the Gadaveri, two of the great rivers of India, which rise on the eastern slope of this watershed, find no outlet to the western sea which is so near to them, but have to traverse hundreds of miles, and cross the whole breadth of India before they lose themselves in the Bay of Bengal. The nearness of these hills is also most beneficial to the inhabitants of Bombay, as they can be used as a sanatorium in the hot weather.

We arrived at Poona after sunset, but as I stopped there ten days I had a good opportunity of seeing the place. Poona is in many ways a typical Indian city and station, and a description of it may serve for many other places in India. Poona then like most other large Indian cities is divided into two parts; viz.: the native city and the British cantonment. These two parts are quite distinct, and the majority of the English residents rarely, if ever, enter the native quarter. The cantonment contains barracks, parade grounds, churches, and streets of detached bungalows (each in its own compound). Here are the Bund gardens, where the English people walk and drive of an evening to "eat the air." Here too is the club, the tennis grounds, the council chamber and public buildings, for Poona is the seat of the Bombay Government during the hot weather, and head-quarters of the Bombay army. The English quarter covers five or six square miles of ground, and in it there are streets of native shops, which sell English goods and also supply all the manifold wants of the Europeans. All this quarter has sprung up within the last 70 years. Poona used to be the capital of the Marhattá power, and the residence of the ruler of the Marhattá confederacy, who was called the Peshwá of Poona. The Peshwá was finally defeated in 1818 at the battle of Kirki, and in that year his dominions were annexed to the Bombay Presidency. Thus the English have not held this place for more than two generations, and the recollection of their independence is still fresh in the minds of the natives. These Marhattás are one of the finest races of India, of a light-brown colour, and very active and manly. They fought as our allies in Southern India, in our wars with Tipu Saib, and are much more independent in manner than the natives of Lower Bengal. The native city is still full of memorials of the greatness of the Peshwá, and many of his old palaces are still standing. If we enter this, we at once see the difference between the English cantonment and the native quarter. Here no Europeans live except a community of the Cowley Fathers. The streets are narrow and unpaved, and full of life. The drive through these streets was a most nervous matter, as everyone walked in the middle of the road, and would hardly move out of the way of a carriage, in spite of the shouts raised by the syce who preceded us. Here one saw native life in perfection. The bazaars were crowded with customers, the fountains at the street corners were surrounded with women drawing water in their brass lotas, who carried naked babies astride on their hips. In the tanks men were washing themselves, there were shops of sweetmeats, and rice, and ghee, full of flies, the native workers in brass and silver were busy with their tools, the potter's wheel whirred in the sunlight, and the little clay vessels were set out to dry, there was a twang from a cotton bow, a murmur of voices and a glimpse of naked children sitting on the floor as we passed an elementary school, while at the division of the ways there stood some idol shrine or figure of a god, daubed with vermilion paint, and generally surrounded with worshippers. The commonest idol in the city seemed to be the Ganapati, or elephant headed idol; he is the god of luck, and typifies cunning or sly cleverness, and is much worshipped by traders. The houses were generally of two stories, the ground floor being given up to the shop, while the upper story was carefully shuttered, and occupied by the women of the household. The shops were mere counters abutting on the street, on which the goods were exposed for sale and on which the owner often sat crosslegged. Within and behind him there were cupboards, from which he would produce further goods, or sometimes there were rooms in which the loom or the lathe was seen at work. By degrees one learned to distinguish the different castes and trades. The Brahmins seemed lighter coloured than the rest, and more aristocratic looking. Here in the Marhattá country the turbans were specially fine, often of red and gold, with a peculiar shell-shaped fold in the centre, which stood up like a horn on the top of the head On every side and down every street there seemed a crowd of life, the population of Poona being over 118,000 people.

We saw the country round Poona by driving in the early mornings. The most interesting sight near the city is the temple of Parvathi. It is dedicated to the consort of Siva, who is here worshipped under the name of Parvathi, which means "mountaineer." It is a picturesque pile of buildings standing boldly upon a high hill three miles outside the town, and built about 150 years ago. There is a silver image of Siva, and others of Vishnu, &c. The Brahmin who showed us over rather mocked at the whole of the worship, but this manner was no doubt partly put on as a compliment to us, and in hopes of obtaining money. This he did not get, as the temple is kept up by Government as a show place. From it there was a magnificent view over the country, and we were shown the window through which the Peshwá watched the battle of Kirki, and saw his troops defeated by the English. Another morning I was taken to see an institution set apart for those suffering from black leprosy. This disease did not appear to be infectious, though it was certainly hereditary. The poor creatures were of all ages, even children inheriting the disease. It showed itself in a hardening of the outer skin, which became like leather, a wasting away of the flesh, and a loss of faculties and also of the limbs. Many were without sight or hearing,—nearly all had some of their toes or fingers rotted away. The joints of the fingers seemed to drop off piecemeal, and one man looked like a walking skeleton, with hardly any flesh, and a thick black leathery hide stretched over his bones. He could neither see nor hear, and hardly speak. The hospital had been founded by a philanthropic Jew. There was no cure for the disease, and the only alleviation possible was to place the sufferers in these alm-houses, where their wants were supplied, and themselves taken care of, till death came to release them from their sufferings.

As soon as the first hunger of sightseeing had been partially satisfied, I began to ask questions about missionary work. One felt one was in an heathen country for the first time in one's life, and one desired to know what progress was being made in converting the natives to Christianity. And at first one got very scant answers. The ordinary official Englishman is too busy with his own work to see much of that of the missionary. Sometimes also he is prejudiced against any attempts to alter the religious feelings of the natives, and will say that the native who becomes a Christian adopts all the vices of the European, while losing the restraints which his former faith imposed upon him. Often also there is some reason for this belief, as the native Christians are not always the best specimens of their race. A certain small number are willing to be converted from very low motives, and these bring discredit on the whole work. Also in former days there was a lack of wisdom shown by certain missionaries, who were ignorant of the religion they meant to overthrow, and thus gained the contempt of the officials, who had lived for many years in the country. Even the chaplains seemed often ignorant of what the missionaries were doing at their own doors. This arises from the chaplain's work being confined to the Europeans dwelling in cantonments, while the missionary works in the native city or in the surrounding villages. Also a chaplain of a large station has plenty to do, having a large number of English, both civil and military, to visit, while the military hospital and soldiers' school have also to be attended to by him. Probably he also has outlying stations, distant often 30 or 40 miles, which he has periodically to visit. All this leaves him but little time to hear much about the missionaries' work. I think the missionaries whom I saw felt a little hurt at the slight interest their own countrymen took in their work. But no doubt the work is strengthened by this lack of official patronage. The converts have nothing to gain in a worldly point of view by becoming Christians, and thus the sincerity of their motives is assured. Since also the official rulers of the country have to treat those professing all religions on an equality, it is perhaps wise that there should be no suspicion of any bias on their part. I can only relate what I saw and heard, but certainly I was agreeably surprised at the quantity and quality of the missionary work. After all that I had heard in depreciation of their labours, I was astonished to find so much knowledge on the part of the missionary, so much wisdom in his methods, and so much solid success attained. It would be an impertinence on my part to praise men wiser and nobler than myself, but I would say to all those (whether in England or in India) who doubt about missionary work, Go and see. Do not be satisfied with hearsay evidence, or current misstatements, or ignorant prejudice, but go down into the native quarter and see the dispensaries, the schools, the orphanages, and the congregations the missionaries have founded, and see if all this does not compare favourably with what is being done in a large London parish. The work seemed to me to be everywhere alive, and the prospect hopeful. There are no doubt careless or unwise missionaries, as there are lazy and ignorant clergymen at home, but I did not meet any, and from what I saw, I was fully convinced of the reality and the progress of mission work. If I try to describe something of what I saw, it may lead others to realize what is being done in this matter.

Poona is a place where nearly all Christian bodies are at work, and the methods used by all of them are much the same. The main parts of the machinery, by which they work on the natives, are orphanages, schools, dispensaries, and open lectures followed by free discussion. The orphanages take in any foundling or deserted children, which are sent to them by the magistrates, and these children are brought up as Christians. The schools are generally open to all of any creed. The dispensaries offer medical advice either gratis or for a small fee, and are means by which acquaintance is made with the sick. The lectures have taken the place of street preaching, which has been given up by many missionaries as being a less effective way of appealing to the people. It would be tedious if I was to enumerate all the different institutions I visited. I give general results gathered from several sources. The orphanages seem useful, for they train up a certain number of infants from childhood in Christian principles; and as these infants are sent to them by Government officials, they seem guarded from the abuse inseparable from all free foundling institutions. The children when fully grown are happily married to children of other Christian orphanages. The sisters of S. Mary's Home (a branch of the Wantage community) told me that they had more applications for wives than they could supply. In the male orphanages the boys are taught trades, such as printing or carpentering, and thus the old reproach that the native Christian was inclined to loaf and live on the missionaries is being removed. When they marry, they live near the mission house, and a Christian community is gradually formed. Right in the heart of the native city of Poona there is such a community rising round the mission house of the Cowley Fathers. These devoted men have not been content to live amongst the other Europeans in cantonments, but they have gone down into the midst of the native quarter, and there live amongst the people. Their house is always open to enquirers, and they receive many visits from natives, more often from curiosity than from a desire to hear about Christianity. Yet these visits often lead to important results, as witness the case of Father Goreh, who was formerly a Brahmin, but is now a Christian and a Cowley Father. He was converted some years ago at Benares, and he himself says that he was in the habit of going to talk to the missionaries for the sake of argument and to improve his English. He now works with the Cowley Fathers at Poona, and is most useful in writing books and tracts, as his knowledge of Brahminism is perfect. But more useful than any other methods are the schools of the missionaries. These are thrown open to all who are willing to come, and there is no compulsion laid on anyone to become a Christian. The heathen lads gladly avail themselves of this privilege, as they know that they will be taught English at these schools. Their great desire is to learn English, as that opens the way to Government employment. And they know also that they will be better taught by a thorough Englishman than they would be by a native teacher. So they willingly come, although they know that their teacher is of a different religion to themselves, and probably will try to convert them. It is in these schools that much of the influence of the missionary is exercised. He does not always try to convert them by compulsory Bible reading or direct dogmatic teaching, for indirect means are often more suitable. Boys naturally look up to the clever and kind European who is instructing them in Western lore, and they are disposed to accept his opinions on all subjects. The very atmosphere of a Christian school and intercourse with a religious-minded man have great influence, even if he does not preach Christianity directly to them. Ideas of Christian morality are insensibly absorbed, and the boy cannot go back to idolatry with his old feelings unshaken. The civilized, clean life of the European with his high notions of truthfulness, and duty, and self-sacrifice, must preach an unspoken sermon, and the constant influence of such a mind must have a great effect on the scholars round him. Therefore there seems every reason to make the missionary schools as efficient and successful as possible, and a great part of the missionary's work will lie in educating the young. His school ought to show as good results in the Government examinations as any other, for this proof of his success will attract more scholars round him. He will consider no time wasted, which is bestowed on secular teaching, for not only does this Western learning sap the old idolatry, but it also acts as a bait by which more of the young are brought under his personal influence. Everyone interested in education seemed to allow that the new learning had sapped the old idolatry, and that the educated natives are now often Atheists or Materialists, though going occasionally to the Temple services. But this destruction of the old religion seems a necessary preliminary to the adoption of the new, and though we may regret the general decay of faith, yet there is nothing to regret in the decay of modern Hinduism. In that religion immorality necessarily forms a part, and one of the indirect benefits of Christianity is that these licentious practices are now condemned by the public opinion of the higher classes of natives, who are being educated up to a purer standard of morality by their contact with Europeans. It is sad to think that the Agnostic and infidel literature of the West finds a ready sale amongst the English speaking Hindus, but even this is better than the old idolatry with its impure rites, and it may even prove a stepping-stone to higher things. Infidelity amongst the educated classes was no barrier to the spread of Christianity in Greece and Rome, and in India the same sequence of events may be repeated; and although a certain number of minds may be content for a time with a blank materialism, yet we may hope that they will emerge from that into a purer faith. The chief hope is in the Christian schools, and from them, if efficiently conducted, may arise a new generation of Christian natives, able to be the evangelizers of their own countrymen. The reading of Shakspeare or Thackeray, of Burke or Johnson, exercises a Christian influence, and thus the very preparation for a Government examination helps forward indirectly the cause of a higher morality and a purer religion.

It may be interesting to state what are the various sorts of schools in India. There are first the Government High Schools, entirely supported by Government funds; these were originally founded as model schools, before any private venture schools had been started. But now in the Bombay Presidency there are several sorts of schools, which have been started privately both by English and native committees, and are aided by Government grants (as in England) subject to inspection. The highest are the European and Eurasian and English teaching schools, which can earn five rupees on each child for average attendance and perhaps twenty-five rupees for every pass made. The pass grant varies, according to the standard passed, increasing as the standard increases. These schools prepare for matriculation, and teach arithmetic, Euclid, algebra, English history, geography, and one other language, either Latin, Sanskrit, French or German. These schools are chiefly attended by the Europeans and Eurasians. Then come the Anglo-vernacular schools, which also prepare for matriculation, but the vernacular language is taught with greater attention to scholarship. Besides that, English, history, geography, Euclid, algebra, Sanskrit or Latin are taught; grants would perhaps average about ten rupees a child, but all through the Indian code the grants increase according to the standard passed, which plan might be introduced with advantage into the English code. Geography and history are made compulsory subjects for the higher standards in all schools. Then there are the vernacular schools, which teach arithmetic, reading, writing and geography in the vernacular. Pupils must have passed in Standard IV. in the vernacular schools before they are permitted to learn English. Each child in these schools would earn about four-and-a-half rupees. . Thus there are schools for every grade of society, but attendance is not compulsory anywhere, so all the children are not being educated. Just before I was at Poona the Education Commission appointed by Government had been holding its sittings. Everyone interested in schools was examined. Hindus, Parsees, Christians, headmasters, mistresses, college officials, missionaries, and magistrates were all invited to give their opinions. They answered certain questions in writing, and were afterwards examined on their evidence. The chief educational question seems to be whether Government should continue to support some schools entirely. They did so at first for the purpose of encouraging education. They also give grants-in-aid to other schools, subject to inspection. But the missionary, and native private venture, schools say that they cannot compete with the Government schools, which are entirely supported out of Government funds. That it would be fairer if Government now discontinued their own schools, and gave a grant-in-aid to any school which passed the required standards: that the present system discourages all sorts of demominational schools, whether Christian or heathen, and that practically the Government is not neutral to all religions, but encourages Atheism; for as it cannot teach any religion, it destroys the old religious belief, without putting anything in its place. They would therefore prefer a system of denominational schools aided by grants (as in England), and would have no more schools entirely supported by Government. On the other hand the Government say that they have no guarantee that the schools to which they give grants-in-aid, will be always continued; that some masters have given up their schools when they had made enough money; and that if they closed their own schools, and only granted aid to private schools, the education of the district might suddenly cease by these schools being shut. There is also no local body fit to be intrusted with the education of the district, for the municipal bodies are hardly yet capable of taking over schools. There was also a fear amongst the Hindus that if the Government closed its schools the missionaries would gain an advantage, since they were already in the field. The private native schools are not yet endowed or generally started. There was a general consensus of opinion that primary village vernacular schools should be multiplied, and that masters and mistresses should be trained for them. There seemed to be a general wish that Government should gradually withdraw from giving any education in its own schools, and should rather confine itself to inspecting. But several said that the time for this had hardly come. Probably with the spread of local self-government this will be gradually effected.

After these rather dry educational questions, it may be interesting to say something about the schools themselves. I had the good fortune to see nearly all the schools in Poona, from the Bishop's high school for English boys down to small orphanages for native infants. I will only mention a few, which had some special points of interest. There was first the Victoria School, which is one of the most interesting in Poona. It is kept by Mr. and Mrs. Surabji and their daughters. He was a Parsee, but was converted to Christianity and ordained a deacon. Mrs. Surabji was a Hindu by birth. Their daughters were helping them, and one had been in England and had been trained at Wantage. The school is specially interesting as one in which natives, and English, and Eurasians, are educated together. Even Hindu girls who are married come to the school. One to whom we spoke was the girl-wife of a man in the service of the Gáekwár of Baroda, and wore the native dress, nose-ring, earrings, and all complete. They had also Mohammedans, Parsees, and Jews, so all sorts and races were there. The wonderful thing is that Hindu girls attend the school. Only a few at present, but still it is a beginning. The children sang Kindergarten songs and were drilled just like a good English school, and we were told that they had done very well in the Government examination. It is one of the first attempts at native female education under English forms, with native teachers. Christianity is taught, but the heathen children are not made to answer, though they are present at the lesson given to the Christian children.

Another interesting experiment was the Government training college for native mistresses. It is kept by Mrs. Mitchell, the widow of a missionary, who has a perfect knowledge of Marhattee. It is entirely secular, and is an attempt to train natives, who are widows or married women, as teachers of native village schools. The young women seemed intelligent and well taught. We saw some beautiful map drawing, and they recited Marhattee poetry.

The largest school I saw was the Government native high school, which was in the centre of the native city, and was accommodated in an old palace of the Peshwás, with carved wooden pillars and ceilings in the rooms, which are built round a quadrangle, and with narrow stair-cases in the thickness of the walls. The first class was preparing for matriculation, and read a piece of Thackeray, and recited from Shakspeare. The teaching seemed good, but the attempt to learn everything seemed to lead to a superficial knowledge and a disposition to rely on primers and condensed abstracts, rather than fuller works. The English spoken was good, grammatical, and well pronounced, and the meaning of English idioms was well explained. This class had lately acted *The Merchant of Venice*, and we asked "Portia," who was a married man about nineteen years old, to give us "The quality of mercy,

&c," which he did with great effect and considerable dramatic power.

I received an invitation from Mr. Kunte, master of the high school, to be present at the breaking up of the school for the Diwali holidays, which I gladly accepted. We arrived about eight o'clock in the morning, and found the whole school assembled, but my brother and I were the only Europeans present. Mr. Kunte received us very cordially, speaking capital English, and full of educational theories, which he was ready to discuss. We had a little talk about the necessity of physical as well as mental training for boys, and we asked about the games his lads played. So he showed us some native gymnastics. The boys stripped naked, except a small waist cloth; their limbs looked hard, muscles well developed, and they were as supple as Greeks. They did some wonderful feats on a vertical pole, swinging themselves round it with their heads downwards, and returning on to their feet with great quickness. Then they showed us some wrestling, which is a great national game amongst the Marhattás. They had a sunk sanded arena, into which two equally matched boys jumped. They fenced a little before they grappled, and challenged each other by clapping their own shoulders with resounding thwacks. When they caught hold, the object of each was to turn his opponent on to his back, but it was not considered a fair fall unless both shoulders touched the ground. All sorts of dodges were allowed; there seemed to be no rules as to holding on to any special part of the body, but they fell, and clung, and twisted, and writhed together as quick, and supple, and agile, and slippery, as possible. Both were panting with the exertion, each trying to gain some hold or advantage, till one was conquered. We saw several pairs thus wrestle, and it gave us a good idea of the physical training given at the school. Then came the English lecture with which the headmaster always closed the term, and for which we were given the chief seats; it was prefaced by a few words of welcome and compliment to us for attending. The title of it was "Machinism," which the lecturer said was an American word. It was very fluent and well expressed. It was intended to answer the question why Englishmen were superior to Hindus. Machinery was specially dwelt upon as the distinguishing point of difference. Yet the lecturer showed that all machines were invented and worked by human means; that Hindus were as capable as Englishmen of inventing and working; that though natural advantages as coal and iron were wanting, yet that much could be done by simpler materials and hand labour. He explained how force was generated, increased, transformed, and applied, and he encouraged them all not to be afraid of machinery, but to educate themselves to use and invent it. He did not want his pupils to become only Government officials, but to learn to earn an independent livelihood. There was a strong vein of nationalism and patriotism running through his speech, and also a good moral tone; he specially enforced on them the necessity of truthfulness. At the end of the lecture I said a few words of compliment, and then cheers were given for him and for me and we came away. He gave me an English book he had written called *The Vicissitudes of Aryan Civilization in India*, and we parted with more pretty speeches. It was altogether a most interesting morning, and he was evidently pleased at Englishmen coming to hear him.

This was nearly my last day at Poona, and I was preparing to start for Rajputana and the North West Provinces. It had been a capital place to begin the study of modern Indian life, for all classes both of European and native people could there be met. One could see how the two races refused to amalgamate, and yet interacted one on the other. The hope of the future seemed to lie in the spread of Western learning, which would supply what was lacking to the Hindu character. As one English-speaking native said to me, "If the English were driven out of India to-morrow, I would fight sword-in-hand for the retention of the English language." He felt that this was the bond which united his race to Western Aryans, and that through English literature his countrymen must gain a higher civilization and a purer morality. All honour then to those, whether missionaries, administrators, or educationalists, who are encouraging the spread of Western learning. We may sometimes be offended by the superficial knowledge and crude ideas of the English-speaking Babu. He may disgust our feelings and shock our taste. He may need to have his faults corrected, and to learn humility, and reticence, and self-control. But with him is bound up the future of India, and his class contains the true elements of progress.

CHAPTER II.

I LEFT Poona on November 6th, 1882, for Rajputana and the North-West. On my way back to Bombay I stopped at Karli station, and walked three miles from there to the famous cave. The walk itself in the early morning was pleasant, and we saw something of agricultural life. The soil seemed rich, and the rice crop was just ripe. In some places the fields were being ploughed, and we noticed how the ploughman

> "Planted both feet upon the leaping share
> To make the furrow deep."

Bullocks were chiefly used to drag the plough, but sometimes they harnessed the great water buffaloes, who looked savage and ill-tempered. The rice crops were partly injured by locusts, and as we passed through the fields great flights of these insects rose on all sides of us. Their bodies were like grasshoppers, and they had four thin gauzy wings like those of a dragon-fly. We had a steep climb up the side of a hill, and then found ourselves opposite a perpendicular face of rock, in which the great cave had been excavated. This cave had been cut out in Buddhistic times. The date assigned to it is A.D. 85, when this style was in its greatest purity, and it is considered one of the finest specimens of the rock hewn temples in India. The general plan of the interior reminded one of a Christian church, only every part was hewn out of the living rock instead of being built up of stone. First there was a richly carved screen, full of figures of men and animals. Entering through this, one found oneself in a long nave, with a row of pillars on either side, supporting a semicircular roof made with wooden rafters, like the ribs of a ship. The pillars are set near together, and are richly carved. The deep shadows between them give a mysterious gloom to the side aisles, and an appearance of depth which is misleading, as the wall of the natural rock lies close behind the pillars. The whole length of the cave is more than 100 feet, and the height about 40 feet. It ends in a semicircular apse, and the pillars are carried round the entire circuit of the walls. At the far end is the shrine, but there is no image or other representation of a god. Only a great circular dome-shaped boss of rock, rising more than half-way up to the roof, perfectly smooth and accurately rounded, which originally supported a wooden umbrella, which was the sign of power, and the only symbol of the Divinity permitted in Buddhistic buildings. The only window is one placed high up in the entrance screen, and thus all the light which enters the temple falls on the shrine, while other parts are left in comparative gloom. Evidently the designer of this cave was a master of effect, and understood how to use shadow, and how to concentrate his light on the most important part of his building. These cave temples are found in various parts of the Bombay Presidency, and in Behar and Cuttack in Bengal. No doubt the natural features of the country determined the districts where this mode of excavation should be employed. It could only be practicable where there existed perpendicular faces of rock of sufficient smoothness and homogeneity to enable the sculptured pillars and figures to be left intact. Any flaw or fault in the rock would spoil the effect of the general design. It is not therefore surprising that these caves are only found in certain parts of India. It has been calculated that it would be less laborious to carve out such a temple than to build one of similar size and of the same material. The labour of removing the tons of rock and leaving the pillars intact would be less toilsome and difficult than the rearing up of these enormous masses and vaulting them over with arched stone roofing. Therefore while we wonder at the skill of these ancient excavators, we may also recognize the fact that they discovered the easiest as well as the most effective way of accomplishing their purpose.

They could never have succeeded in arching over such large spaces with stone, but by using, and enlarging, and embellishing natural caves they succeeded in overcoming all difficulties, and thus left enduring monuments of their skill almost indestructible by time. We walked back from the cave to Karli station, and there took the train to Bombay, and on that same evening I left by the mail train for Baroda. The distance is 247 miles, and I arrived about 4 a.m.

Railway travelling in India presents some special features of interest to the English passenger. The carriages are built with double roofs, and overhanging eaves, so that the passengers are protected from the fierce heat of the sun. There are four classes on most Indian lines. The first-class carriages are occupied chiefly by the covenanted civilians, ladies, and the richer native gentry. In the second-class carriages one finds the younger civilians, policemen, railway officials, and Eurasians; besides native merchants, babus, Parsees and others. The intermediate class (between the second and the third) is used by the poorest Englishmen. While the cheapest class of all is almost solely used by natives. These form the majority of the passengers. There will be four times as many third class carriages in a train as any other, and every carriage will be quite full. The third-class fares are very low, and the natives have taken very willingly to this mode of conveyance. Pilgrimages are now performed by means of the railway, and when any great feast, or holiday, or sacred anniversary is at hand, special trains have to be run to accommodate the crowds of passengers. Every platform is filled with travellers, the ground outside the station is covered with prostrate forms rolled up in rugs, sleeping on the bare earth, waiting for the train to start, and the noise and confusion is appalling. Even on an ordinary day the number of native passengers is very surprising. They do not carry much luggage, generally only a small bundle. The women are loaded with bangles, having apparently disposed all their jewelry about their persons. And the black-eyed children cling round their mothers, sitting astride on their hips. The stationmasters are generally natives, while the guards and engine-drivers are Eurasians. The latter are clothed in white uniforms and wear "sola topees," or pith hats. At every station there are two bhîstis, or water carriers, who serve out water gratis to all who ask for it. One of these is a Hindu, and the other is a Mohammedan, and each serves the passengers of his own faith. The Hindu water carrier is always chosen from a high caste, as it would be pollution for a high-caste native to accept water from a low-caste water carrier. The cry of "páni, páni" (water, water) is the first thing one notices at the wayside stations. There are also sellers of bananas, cocoa-nuts, sweetmeats, bread, and rice, who pass up and down the platforms crying their wares. The wants of the Europeans are also well attended to, and the trains stop sufficiently long to allow time for meals, while the guard telegraphs on to inform the butler at the next refreshment room how many passengers require breakfast or dinner. The meals are good, and the charges are not excessive. The carriages are well arranged for night travelling, as the seats are easily converted into shelves or bunks, on which one can lie at full length. There is a lavatory attached to each carriage, where one can wash and brush up, and the guards do not wake one up when asleep with a demand for tickets. The lines are terribly dusty, and one arrives covered with grit, and coal dust, and sand. Fortunately a bath is always quickly ready, and after washing one is more presentable. The hospitality of Indian residents is proverbial, and though now hotels are more common, and there is not the same necessity for taking in the casual traveller, yet still their kindness is excessive. I have a great debt of kindness to acknowledge, and I cannot sufficiently express my gratitude to those who laid themselves out to make my Indian tour pleasant. Indian houses seemed to be elastic, and there was always room made somehow for one person more. If the house was full, a tent was pitched in the compound, and one slept under canvas. This was most luxurious, as the furniture of an Indian tent would bear comparison with many an English bedroom. There was a thick carpet on the floor, the bed was covered with a bright red rezai, there was a pretty dressing table decked with flowers, and lit with wax candles, a bath tent was attached with plenty of water carried in by the attendant bhîsti, and outside there marched a sentinel to watch over one's slumbers. The nights at this time of the year (November) were delightfully cool, and I was never visited by snake or scorpion. I was always glad when I heard that my friends had arranged a tent for me. It did not seem a matter for apology, but rather for congratulation. The being awakened in the early morning by the song of birds, the first glimmer of dawn through the tent door, the sounds of drawing water at the well, the early cup of tea brought in by the bearer, and the morning walk before breakfast, are all pleasurable memories. Later on in the day it was unwise to go out, and from eleven o'clock till four one stopped indoors, and read and wrote. But after afternoon tea a drive or a walk, a game of tennis or a spell of sightseeing became possible. The English community in India at the smaller stations is obliged to be friendly. They are necessarily so much thrown together, that they cannot be distant or haughty. They try to discover each other's good points and to ignore as far as possible any faults which may exist. They are either great friends or else deadly enemies, and it is not often that the latter state is reached. The chief difficulty is occupation for the English ladies, as the heat prevents out-of-door work of all kinds. The less educated become gossipy and foolish, caring much for admiration, and spending much time in dressing and visiting. But in most stations there are now good libraries, the magazines and newspapers arrive each week from England, and it is possible for anyone in India to keep himself abreast of English thought, and to be as cultured and well educated as anyone living in the centre of intellectual life at home.

My stay at Baroda was made pleasant for me through the kindness of the Resident. The State of Baroda is one of those feudatory states which is governed by a native Prince, with the help and advice of an English Resident, who is appointed by the Viceroy. The Resident does not interfere in the internal government of the state, unless he notices any grave abuses. He is always ready to advise the native ruler, and he has the power of exercising a control over the foreign relationships of the state. The power of life and death is exercised by the native Prince, though the Resident would forbid any extreme act of injustice. Thus the position of a Resident at a native court is one of great responsibility and delicacy. He has to make friends with the ruler, and yet to keep himself free from all palace intrigues. He has to exercise a wise oversight, and yet to avoid all fussy interference. He has to know when it is needful to speak, but he does not continually meddle with the small details of internal government. He is in the State, yet not of it, and behind him there is known to be the whole power of the British Empire, though this fact is not flaunted in the face of the native ruler. He must be careful not to offend any native susceptibilities, and he tries to occupy the position of a friendly helper rather than that of a powerful intruder. He makes his favourable opinion a matter to be desired, while his displeasure is proportionately feared. He is able to show his feelings on any subject by his tone and manner, while keeping in reserve the more distinct expressions of praise or blame. He studies to win by every means in his power the confidence of the ruler to whose court he is attached, and yet retains his own independence of life, so that he can at any time interfere if occasion requires. In the majority of cases years may elapse without there being any call for the exercise of a Resident's veto, but we need strong men at these posts, who will be able to act with firmness if an emergency should arise. In 1874 such an emergency arose in Baroda. An attempt was made to poison the then Resident, and the reigning Prince (here called the Gáekwár), Mulhar Rao, was accused of being privy to the crime. He was put on his trial before a commission consisting of three European and three native gentlemen, and the charge was considered sufficiently proved to call for his deposition. He was therefore removed from the throne, and banished from his dominions. But the English Government refrained from annexing the state, and allowed the widow of Khundar Rao, the preceding Gáekwár, to adopt an heir to the throne, as she had no children of her own. Khundar Rao was the elder brother of Mulhar Rao, and Mulhar was suspected of poisoning him in order to obtain the throne. While the present Gáekwár was a minor the state was governed by a native prime minister. An English tutor was appointed to the young Gáekwár, who has thus been educated in English manners. He was placed on the throne a few years ago, and so far he has proved an excellent Prince. Courteous, industrious, upright and energetic, His Highness tries hard to do his duty towards his subjects, and is praised by all who know him. He plays lawn tennis, and will mix in English society, though his caste prevents him from eating with Europeans. He has married a daughter of the Rajah of Tanjore, and still reads English with his tutor, though he is now no longer *in statu pupillari*. The extent of his territory is about 4400 square miles, and the total population over two millions. He has founded a college, where his subjects are well educated, and he is building a large new palace. The city of Baroda is thoroughly native, the streets being very narrow and crowded with people. The Gáekwár possesses some curious gold and silver cannon, and these when used are dragged by great bullocks, the breed in this part of India being specially fine, of a pale buff colour, and with long slender horns. But the most curious survival of bygone days is the great sanded arena where wild beasts are set to fight for the amusement of the spectators. Elephants and tigers, rhinoceroses and rams, are matched against each other, and the scene is said to be exciting, though somewhat cruel. The arena is a large rectangular area about 80 yards long by 40 wide, and numbers of English come from Bombay to see the sight, when the beasts are brought out to make sport (?) for the crowd. Baroda is, I believe, the only native court where this custom survives, and it might perhaps be more honoured in the breach than in the observance.

From Baroda I went north by the Rajputana-Malwa line to Ajmere, which is 367 miles by rail from Baroda, and the capital of a British province, some 50 miles square, which lies in the centre of the Rajput states. These states acknowledged our power as paramount in 1818, and are now feudatory to the British Government. Their position is peculiar in many ways, and Sir A. Lyall has written an essay on their sociology in his *Asiatic Studies*. The Rajputs are supposed to have descended from a Scythian people, who invaded India about 57 B.C., but they soon adopted the Hindu religion. At one time they reigned over nearly the whole of Northern India, but they were driven out by the advance of the Mohammedan power. To escape from these fierce invaders, the Rajputs occupied the deserted plains and hill forts of the district now called Rajputana. Clan by clan they set up for themselves, and refused to bow their necks beneath the yoke of the Moguls. The natural difficulties of the country helped them to retain their independence, and even the most victorious of the Delhi emperors were disinclined to attack these obstinate highlanders. The siege of one of their hill forts was a difficult enterprise, and a victory was sometimes hardly more satisfactory than a defeat. For there are instances mentioned that when the Rajput garrison was finally forced to surrender, they clothed themselves in saffron garments, and drunk with the blood of their women, who had immolated themselves rather than be touched by rude hands, they set their fort on fire and then charged down sword in hand on their besiegers. There was no honour or glory to be obtained by attacking a people who might act like this. The Emperor Akbar tried to conciliate the clans, and intermarried with some of them, but the oldest families still boast that no daughter of their house was ever sent into the harem of the great Mogul. The Rajput clans were formed after the manner of swarms of bees. When the ancestral halls became too strait for the numerous scions of the house, one would go forth with a following of relations and would carve a new home for himself out of the lands occupied by aboriginal tribes, and build himself a fort which would become the capital of a new state. All the blood relations of the chief would claim a voice in the government of the state. He would be *primus inter pares*, but they had to be consulted, and their blood was as blue as his. They might even depose him, and appoint another member of the family to be the chief. This original constitution has been modified by time, and since we have overruled the states, the internal government by the whole clan has been superseded. We have recognized the chief of the clan as the reigning Prince, and we have called the other members of the clan his nobles. But originally the constitution was less despotic, and the whole clan claimed to have a voice in the government of the state. The whole of Rajputana is thus subdivided amongst several clans, varying in numbers, and in extent of territory. Before the English Government established a permanent peace, these clans were constantly fighting amongst each other, and the retainers of different chieftains could hardly meet without bloodshed. Even now there are intertribal jealousies, which render Durbars, and other state ceremonials, very difficult matters; for the question of precedence of one chieftain over the other is debated as fiercely as it used to be of old in the Scottish Highlands.

The peculiar constitution of the Rajput states has led the British Government to try an experiment for the higher education of the young nobles of these ancient houses. Mayo College, which is to be the Eton of India, has been established just outside the town of Ajmere. Each state in Rajputana is allowed to build a house for its own boys. So in a park near the town there stand a number of detached houses, of different styles yet all most beautifully built, each capable of holding from 10 to 20 boys. The lads come at any age from 7 to 18, but no one is admitted unless he belongs to a family whose chief would have a right to a seat in the Viceroy's Durbar. Their physical education is specially attended to, they are obliged to keep horses, and are taught to ride, and they play at cricket and lawn tennis. They are bound to learn English and Urdu, as these are the two languages of polite intercourse, but the whole object of their training is to make them gentlemen rather than scholars. There are now about 50 boys in the school, and the Principal is helped by two English masters, besides numerous pundits. The difficulty is to prevent jealousies between scions of different houses and whilom hostile dynasties, and to cut down the retinue which these lads desire to bring with them. Each boy has a separate study, which he is allowed to decorate as he pleases with photographs and pictures. They seemed pleased to show their rooms, and were pleasant spoken, bright faced, clean-looking lads. The discipline seemed excellent. No boy is allowed outside the bounds of the park without leave, and there is a resident care-taker in each house, who is responsible to the Principal for its internal economy. No attempt is made to alter their religion, and an offer lately made by a private individual to build a temple for their use has been accepted. The central building, which is to contain class rooms and lecture halls, is not yet finished. It is being most beautifully built of different coloured marbles, which are found in quarries in the neighbourhood, and the central hall, when finished, will be one of the handsomest rooms in India. The boys trained here are likely to do well. One of the old scholars is the present Rajah of Ulwar, who is highly spoken of, and as time goes on more of the lads will be reigning princes. Certainly the education they are receiving here is far superior to the old harem training, which was all that they formerly received, and Mayo College is likely to prove its usefulness in every one of the Rajput states.

The town of Ajmere is well worth a visit. It stands in a valley encircled by hills, and has its walls and flanking towers still standing. The hill above the town is crowned by a fort, said to have been built by the Emperor Akbar. One side of the town is bounded by a beautiful lake, about five miles in circumference, along the banks of which rise marble palaces and open loggias, with pillared balconies overhanging the water, the waves of which lap with a cool and pleasant sound against the white walls of these luxurious residences. It is in Ajmere that one first begins to realize the greatness of the Mogul Emperors, whose magnificent architectural triumphs are the wonder of Delhi and Agra. For in Ajmere they had their summer residences, and occupied these palaces on the borders of the lake, when the heat became too great to remain in the capital. This also accounts for the strong way in which Ajmere was fortified, for it lay in the midst of the hostile Rajput states, and was ever liable to attack. Here we see remains of the way in which these Mohammedan rulers strove to change the religion of their Hindu subjects. In the midst of Ajmere there rises the Durgah, a marble mosque, built over the silver shrine of a Mohammedan saint, who came to Ajmere in 1235 A.D., and which is considered so sacred that all men (including Europeans) have to remove their boots before entering in at the gate. But the most interesting building is just outside the walls of the town. Passing through one of the numerous fortified gates, and ascending the slope of the Taragarh hill, one comes to the Arhai-din-ka-Jhonpra mosque, so called because it was said to have been built in two-and-a-half days or *arhai-din*. Here originally stood an old Jain temple, built some 1800 years ago. The Jains were a religious sect, who started contemporaneously with the Buddhists, and held similar doctrines. The movement was one in opposition to caste distinctions and the power of the Brahmins. When the Mohammedan conqueror saw this building, he desired that it should be made fit for him to worship in. So he ordered a splendid façade to be erected in front of the old temple, and this according to the legend was done in two-and-a-half days. Probably that was the time taken by the Mohammedans to deface and destroy the images of gods and saints to which they objected. Both the Jain and the Mohammedan work are splendid specimens of their respective styles. The Jain temple consists of some 40 columns tall and slender; each set of four columns supports a roof made of concentric circles of stone, and these all joined together make a rich and gorgeous canopy. For every edge and fringe of stone is carved with rich patterns and interlaced designs, every pillar is covered with carving, no two being alike, and the figures and ornamentation exist in the richest profusion. The Mohammedan architects, who added a gateway to this temple, have vied with the older builders. Their façade consists of a front of five Saracenic arches, placed as an entrance to the temple, and round each tall arch there are cut Arabic texts from the Korân, superimposed on an underlying lacework pattern in stone, which covers every part of the surface of the façade with ornament. It is the richest piece of stonework carving I have seen, and the conjunction of the two styles in one building adds greatly to the interest of the place.

Ajmere is the head-quarters of the Rajputana State Railway. This has caused a number of railway officials to live there, and several workshops have been opened. These give employment to a number of Eurasians, who act as guards and engine-drivers, engineers and fitters. The springing up of this colony has caused the question of church accommodation and the need of a railway chaplain to come to the front. All over India, since the starting of railways, this question has called for solution. In the old days, if the troops and the covenanted civilians were provided with chaplains and churches, the needs of the European population were sufficiently met. But now in all parts of India there are numbers of Englishmen who have come out as planters or merchants, and are unattached to any branch of the Government service. There are also a number of English artizans in the Government employ; besides a constantly increasing body of Eurasians, the offspring of English fathers and native mothers. It is impossible to ignore the spiritual or temporal needs of this mixed race. For a long time they were overlooked by the Government chaplains, and did not come into the purview of the missionary. And being thus neglected, and feeling that they were despised by both natives and Europeans, what wonder if some of them did not bear the highest characters. A common saying was that the Eurasian had the faults of both races and the virtues of neither, and hearing himself thus described, he sometimes did his best to justify this bad opinion. With the spread of railway works a new profession has been thrown open to him. He makes an admirable guard and engine-driver, as his mixed blood enables him to stand the heat of the climate, while his English parentage gives him more decision and presence of mind in the hour of danger than is possessed by the native of India. And also, since he has thus become a most useful member of the community, his spiritual needs have been more considered. Railway churches and railway chaplains are now established in all centres of population, and the Eurasian can no longer say "that no man cares for his soul." Everyone must rejoice that the Church has thus awoke to the duty she owes to this large section of her members.

From Ajmere I went by train to Jeypore, 84 miles further to the northward. This city is the capital of the native state of that name, and is said to be the best managed city under native rule in India. The early history of the state is mixed up with that of Delhi. It was conquered by the Mogul emperors, but regained its independence when the empire began to decline, in the beginning of the 18th century. The present capital owes much of its beauty to the late Maharajah, who was a very enlightened and well-educated Prince. The town compares favourably with many of those which are under direct British rule. The streets are wide and well paved, lighted with gas (which is a great rarity in India), and the houses are built in regular lines. The majority are stuccoed over, and painted a strawberry-cream colour, with designs in white paint. The whole city is surrounded by a wall, 20 feet high and 9 feet thick, and the neighbouring hills are crowned with forts, which look almost inaccessible. But the late Maharajah did not only care for the defence of his capital; he also studied to improve it in every way. He founded hospitals, built schools, opened a museum, laid out public gardens, and started a school of art for the improvement of native manufactures. Jeypore is famous for its inlaid arms and shields, its beautiful enamel, only workable on a foundation of the purest gold, and its work in precious stones. All these industries were fostered by this enlightened Prince, whose loss was deplored by all who knew him. He had no children, and the present Maharajah was his adopted son. Unfortunately this adoption did not take place till near the end of the late

Prince's life, as like many other sovereigns he was somewhat jealous of his successor. The present Maharajah being thus kept in ignorance of the fate in store for him, received no education, and was raised from a condition of great poverty to the state cushion. He is, however, willing to listen to the advice of the English Resident at his Court, and he may yet do well. He reigns over two-and-a-half millions of people, his territory consists of 13,000 square miles, and there are 800 nobles of his clan, who look on him as *primus inter pares*.

I was curious to see how such a man lived, and I was therefore anxious to see the inside of the Palace. The Court was in mourning on account of the death of the widow of the late Maharajah, so there was no chance of an interview with his Highness. For until the funeral rites were fulfilled, he, as chief mourner, was forced to sit and sleep on the ground, and etiquette forbade him to receive any visitors. He might neither eat sweets nor drink wine, but was obliged to pass the time in seclusion and fasting. But through the kindness of one of the English officials I was shown something of the interior of the Palace, and thus got a glimpse of native court life. The Palace buildings cover one-seventh of the whole area of the city, and are surrounded by a high wall. Within this wall resides the Maharajah's household. There are streets of houses occupied by numerous retainers, guard-rooms and stables, armouries and barracks, and in the centre of all, in the midst of a great court-yard, there rises a pyramidal pile of buildings, many storied, of irregular outline and no particular design, which is the residence of the Maharajah himself. Round the doors of this building and in all the courts and passages there lounged troops of servants, quantities of idle soldiers, every sort and description of household retainer. It reminded one of a great castle in the Middle Ages, when a nobleman's retinue numbered hundreds of lances and the household consisted of scores of servants. We passed at first through low passages into great halls of audience, where the Maharajah could receive numbers of his subjects. The handsomest of these, called the Dewân-i-Khâs, was built entirely of white marble. Above on the higher stories there were the more private reception rooms, gorgeously decorated with glass and ormolu. On every side there was a lavish display of large mirrors, painted ceilings, old carpets, and decorated walls. The taste was often rather barbaric, the brightest colours were most appreciated, and there was often an incongruity visible in the internal decorations. But the amount of money lavished on the furniture and decoration of the building was beyond my computation. As we ascended higher, we reached at last a flat terrace roof overlooking the gardens of the palace, where there was an open pavilion, giving most extensive views. Behind there was the Zenana, with the private apartments, enclosed by high walls, which could not be overlooked. We were shown the armoury, with a splendid collection of inlaid arms, and a choice assortment of hookahs with wondrous mouthpieces and richly wrought bowls. There was a library also with old illuminated manuscripts full of pictures and rich with gorgeous borders; they were chiefly Persian poems and ancient chronicles. There were hardly any staircases in the building, but long inclined passages in the thickness of the walls led from one storey to another. The reason of this is that the Maharajah likes to be carried everywhere in a sedan chair: they say he is growing fat for want of exercise, and is inclined to be lazy. As we descended, we were followed by troops of curious domestics, but were everywhere courteously received, and shown all the wonders of the place. It gave one some insight into the private life of a native ruler. One understood better what was meant by "palace intrigues," "harem influences," "jealousy of successors," and other terms, which make up the history of many an Eastern state. In such a palace as this, which was like a town within a town, there would be room for secret crimes, family quarrels, opposing parties, and rebellious conspiracies. Dynasties might be overthrown, a favourite officer, or a scheming widow, might buy the support of the army, and the unwitting inhabitants of the city or state might suddenly find themselves under a new ruler. All such schemes and plots are impossible now, since the British power has become paramount. These independent princes are no longer capable of rebellion, neither can their rule be overthrown by palace intrigues. The interior of such a palace is no longer a hotbed of mischief, where villainous schemes are brought to maturity. But the atmosphere of the place helped one to realize what used to happen in bygone days, and it was well worth seeing in order that one's historical sense might be enlightened.

We made a most interesting expedition to the old town of Ambir, which is about six miles from Jeypore. This city was finally deserted about 60 years ago, because the surrounding hills prevented its expansion. It was a strongly fortified city, and a most suitable site for the capital of the state in ancient days, but it did not prove as satisfactory for modern needs and more peaceful times. Therefore the new town of Jeypore was founded, and the old capital was deserted. We drove along a well metalled road through an open country, until we came to the foot of a hill, where the carriage stopped. The ascent was too steep for our horses, so we exchanged our conveyance for the back of an elephant. This creature took us the rest of the way, which was about one-and-a-half miles more. He was slow and uncomfortable, and one was not sorry when the ride came to an end. The way an elephant walks is by moving his two legs on the same side together, and this communicates a see-saw motion to the riders, which is rather like the pitching of a small boat in a chopping sea. As his pace is about two-and-a-half miles an hour, he is not an animal to be recommended for those who are in a hurry. However an elephant is wonderfully sure-footed, and no other animal could have carried us so safely up the paths we had to go. The first ascent was not very steep, but that carried us over the brow of the hill, which enclosed the valley, in which Ambir is built. As we descended the opposite slope, we had a beautiful view of the whole spot. In the middle was a lake with a island temple, and inhabited by sacred crocodiles. All round this lake rise steep hills, which encircle it in narrow bounds, except on the northern side where there was a narrow defile, which was the only plain entrance to this secluded valley. Half-way up the hill on one side of the lake there rose the white walls of the old palace, protected by watch-towers, and only to be approached by a narrow winding path. And far above that there is a strong fort, built on the highest hill top, with steep scarped sides, and flanking walls, which connected it with the palace. This must have been the final resort of the clan, when the besiegers from Delhi had taken all their other defences. Our elephant carried us safely up the winding path, and through the gates into the palace courtyard There we dismouted, and were shown over the old halls and rooms, which had once been the residence of the Maharajahs of Jeypore. The marble carved work is most beautiful, and in the Zenana quarters there is some pierced screen stonework which is very rich. From the highest battlements we looked sheer down on to the lake below, from the shores of which the walls seemed to rise almost perpendicularly. We could see the dimensions of the whole valley, and could understand how impossible it was for a large city to grow up in these narrow limits, and how necessary it was to transfer the capital to a more suitable site. Still it will be a great pity if Ambir is ever allowed to fall into ruins, for its picturesque position must be admired by all who see it.

This finished my glimpse at the feudatory states,

and from Jeypore I travelled on to Delhi. But I had got some idea of the curious position in which these native princes stand to the paramount power. They are supreme in their own dominions, yet are overshadowed by the British Resident. They are prevented from foreign aggression, yet have full liberty of action within the limits of their states. Nearly two-fifths of the total area of India is within the borders of the native states. The area of feudatory India is 604,590 square miles, while that of British India is 880,098 square miles. But the population in the native states is only 54 millions, while that in British India is 186 millions. Thus the numbers to the square mile living in the territory we administer are nearly three times as many as those living in native states. This arises partly from the fact that we possess the most fertile portions of India, and partly from the greater security enjoyed under our rule. The provinces most recently annexed by us (*e. g.*, Burma) have increased greatly in population since our rule was established. This seems to disprove the opinion, often expressed, that the natives of India prefer a native ruler, and dislike the British system. Certainly statistics seem to prove the opposite, as they show that the mass of the population crowd within our borders, while the native states are under populated. Dr. W. W. Hunter, in his *Indian Empire*, expects that, as we enforce good government under the native chiefs of India, there will be a gradual movement of the people into the feudatory states. This will be a satisfactory result, (although some English officials may regard the migration with pain); as the population requires to be more equally distributed and relief given to the congested districts. Certainly not the least benefit the British rule has brought to India is the good government exercised not only in British territory, but also in native states, under native rulers, advised by English Residents.

CHAPTER III.

FROM Jeypore to Delhi the railway runs through a thinly populated country, the soil being covered with thickets of pampas grass, and peacocks may be seen in the jungle. The villages become more numerous as Delhi itself is approached. That city is interesting in many ways. Founded originally by Hindus, it has been besieged and taken by the successive invaders of India, for several centuries it was the capital of the Mohammedan Empire, and its name will ever be associated with Mutiny reminiscences. Thus, as in Rome, one is continually passing from mediæval history to modern events; ancient mosques attract one's attention side by side with the spot where the city gate was blown open and Nicholson fell. The British soldier keeps guard in the fort which the great Mogul erected, and memories of far distant times jostle for recognition with stories of the Empress Durbar in 1877. Thus it is difficult to prevent oneself from being bewildered with the diversity of the sights clamouring for attention. But the main interest of Delhi clusters round the great names of the Mogul Emperors, and a short history of these may fitly preface the description of their capital. The first Mohammedan invaders of India were Túrkis and Afghans, but these early invaders only established themselves in the Punjab, and their capital city was Gházni, within the borders of Afghanistan. The Mohammedan generals, who acted as provincial rulers in India, gradually made themselves independent, and in 1206 Kutub-ud-din, an Indian Viceroy, who had originally been a Túrki slave, seized the supreme power and settled in the old city of Delhi, where he built the Minar, which still bears his name. He was the first of the resident Mohammedan sovereigns of India. About 1300 A.D. we first hear of invasions by the Moguls, who were a Tartar tribe living in Central Asia. The great Mogul invasion was in 1398, when Timur (Tamerlane) swept through the Afghán passes at the head of the united hordes of Tartary, defeated King Mahmúd under the walls of Delhi,* and finally retired again into Central Asia, leaving no traces of his power save desolate cities. After his invasion India was divided among a number of local Mohammedan kings and Hindu princes, and Delhi was no longer the capital of an empire. But in 1526 there was a second Mogul invasion, when Bábar founded the dynasty which reigned for three centuries at Delhi, and whose last representative died a British state prisoner in Rangoon in 1862. The greatest of these Mogul emperors was Akbar, who reigned from 1556 to 1605, and was therefore a contemporary of Queen Elizabeth. His empire extended from Afghanistan across all India to Orissa. He removed the capital from Delhi to Agra and built Futtehpore Sikri. His great desire was to conciliate all his subjects. His favourite wife was a Rajput princess, and another is said to have been a Christian. He received the Jesuit Fathers at his Court, and his religion appears to have been of a very eclectic character. Akbar was succeeded by Jehanghir, who reigned from 1605 to 1627. And he in turn was succeeded by his son Shah Jehan, who reigned till 1658. This emperor was the great architect of his time, and it is his buildings which are the wonder and delight of all travellers in India. The Taj Mahál, and the Moti Musjid at Agra, are perhaps the most beautiful buildings in the world, while the palace at Delhi, and the Jumma Musjid, are the great sights of that city. Shah Jehan was succeeded by Aurangzeb, who reigned from 1658 to 1707, but the greatness of the Mogul Empire was then on the wane. The Hindus were beginning

* Hunter's *Indian Empire*, p. 230.

to rise against their oppressors, and the Marhattá power was already formidable. The Rajputs were also in constant revolt, and thus the great Empire was being overthrown. The later history of the Moguls is one of continual disaster, and steady decline. The Persians, the Afghans, and the Marhattás, each in turn invaded their dominions. The later emperors were mere puppets in the hands of victorious generals or ambitious statesmen. Gradually the English built up a new power out of the wreck of the Mogul Empire; the last descendant of Akbar emerged for a moment as a rebel in 1857, and died as a state prisoner in Rangoon in 1862. So passed away the great Mohammedan Empire in India. It had begun to decline before the Marhattá power prior to the advance of the English into Upper India. It has left as its chief relics the magnificent buildings of Agra and Delhi, and a recollection of an Empire consisting of many provinces and many religions, all subject to one paramount power. That empire we have in one sense imitated, and it was a true instinct which led Lord Lytton to choose Delhi as the place where the Queen of England should be proclaimed Empress of India. There on the historic "ridge," where the British army had been encamped for three long months in 1857, from whence the final assault had been delivered which once more made us masters over India, there from a spot overlooking the old capital of the Mogul Emperors, in a Durbar of unparalleled magnificence, attended by feudatory princes, and with every sign and token of power, the empire of the English was proclaimed. But it is to be hoped that we shall take warning as well as example from those old Mogul Emperors lest we fall as they did. Their weakness arose from the hatred with which they were regarded by their subjects, and this hatred sprang from the intolerant and cruel character of their rule. The Hindus were despised and persecuted, and they at last rose and shook off their oppressors. If all the Mogul Emperors had been as conciliatory and sympathetic as Akbar, their rule might have lasted for a longer time. But their subjects hated them, and when the opportunity offered they cast them off. We have to remember that we are in India for the good of the natives, that our rule must be for their advantage, or we have no right to remain. Thus and thus only, if we reign in the hearts of the people, can we hope to exist longer than that old Mogul Empire. There are still more than forty millions of Mohammedans in India. Some of these might be able to trace their descent back to the first Mohammedan invaders. But the majority would be descended from those who changed their religion from fear or for gain when that creed was professed by the Mogul Emperors. Many of them have stood aloof and have refused to take service under us. They have been less adaptive than the Hindus, and have been less ready to qualify themselves for Government employment. They have been less careful to educate their children in English learning, and have thus been outstripped by the nimbler-minded Hindus, who have nearly monopolised the offices given by the Government to natives. Now there is a great stirring amongst the Mohammedans, they are paying more attention to education, and are agitating for equal employment with the other natives of India. If they qualify themselves, there will be no objection made on the score of their religion. The Government only desire to obtain the best men, and all creeds are allowed to compete. But it is foolish for the Mohammedans to complain of the number of Hindus employed by Government, when they take no pains to qualify themselves for the offices thrown open to all the natives of India.

Delhi is a city of over 150,000 inhabitants, and has many objects of interest which could only be properly described in a guide book written for the purpose. I can only hope to mention a few of the sights in this interesting city, which specially remain engraved on my memory. The first thing one notices is the Mohammedan appearance of the city. There are more mosques, fewer Hindu temples, fewer men with caste marks on their foreheads, than elsewhere. And next one notices what a strong place it must have always been, and what a difficult matter the siege of such a fortress was in the days of the Mutiny. The whole city is surrounded by a wall of red granite, five-and-a-half miles in circuit, and in this wall there are twelve great gates, each strongly fortified. Besides this outer wall of defence there is the inner fort, where the Emperor's palace stood, which extends for a mile along the river bank, and is also strongly fortified. It seems marvellous that an English army of 8000 men could have ever besieged and stormed such a city and fortress, when defended by 30,000 trained soldiers. In the city itself there is one main street, which all travellers visit, which is called the Chandi Chowk; it is a mile long, broad, and planted with a double row of trees, and in it are the chief shops, and many public buildings. But the chief interest of Delhi must centre in the fort or palace, where the great Mógul lived and reigned, and in the embellishment of which the whole resources of the empire were lavishly poured forth. Built by Shah Jehan, its glories were for a long time unseen by European eyes. Those who were admitted within its gates only saw a little of its beauty, for the private apartments and women's quarters were kept secret from all prying visitors. In the later days of the empire, when the Emperor existed in name but had no real power, the palace was a sink of iniquity, a home for secret intrigues and dark crimes, a sanctuary for evil, where criminals could lie concealed and escape from justice. Now all parts of this palace are thrown open, many of the buildings which formerly crowded the interior have been removed to make room for barracks, and the only parts left standing are those which are intrinsically beautiful. Entering through one of the great gates, one passes through a long vaulted aisle, like that of a Gothic cathedral, which opens into the central quadrangle within the walls. Here stands the Dewan-i-am, or Hall of Public Audience, open on three sides, supported by numerous red sandstone pillars, and containing a white marble throne, which the Emperor could reach by a door opening out of his private apartments. Beyond this great hall there is the Dewan-i-khas, or Hall of Private Audience. Here instead of sandstone all is built of white marble beautifully polished and enriched with inlaid patterns of gold and precious stones. The richness and gorgeousness of this work defies description. The white marble shines in the light of the Indian sun, and the roof and pillars look almost transparent. The back of this hall overlooks the river Jumna. There are balconies projecting over the riverbed, and one looks down some 60 feet of perpendicular wall, which made this side of the palace quite impregnable. Adjoining the Dewan-i-khas on one side was the seraglio, also of white marble with inlaid designs, and on the other were the baths. These also are of white marble, and in the centre of each room there is a marble bath, sunk in the floor, while all round the room there runs a pattern of colour, made of precious stones, inlaid in the surface of the marble. Near to this stands the Moti Musjid, or Pearl Mosque, a small, but exquisite building, also of white marble, which probably was used by the Emperor's household as their place of worship. It is impossible for me to describe the beauty of these marble halls, overlooking the broad bed of the Jumna, and rich with coloured patterns, and inlaid with gold. All are now empty and deserted. The English sentry keeps watch at the gate, and one or two chance sightseers are all that are visible. Every care seems taken of the buildings, and they are so strongly built that there seems no fear of their decay.

Leaving the palace, and crossing the road one comes opposite to the great Jumma Musjid, or "Friday Mosque." This is one of the most striking objects in Delhi, its minarets are visible for miles round, and its size and sacredness render it a great resort of worshippers. It was built by Shah Jehan, and it took ten years to complete. It is a typical example of the mode of arrangement of all mosques, and a description of its internal plan may explain the idea of all Mohammedan places of worship. It is built on a flat raised terrace of red sandstone, which lifts the building high above the street. This terrace or platform is reached by three handsome flights of steps, which lead up to three great gateways, one in the centre of each wall. Entering by the eastern gateway, which is more splendid than the others, one finds oneself in a large courtyard or quadrangle open to the sky. In the centre is a marble reservoir for water, used for ablutions by the worshippers, and round the court-yard there runs an open colonnade, with towers at the angles. The floor is paved with white marble, and the faithful Islamites leave their shoes at the entrance. Opposite the great gate and across the court-yard is the mosque itself. This is a building made of white marble and crowned with three bulbous-shaped domes. Its interior is fully exposed to view, as the arches by which it is entered are very lofty. It is paved with long slabs of white marble bordered with black lines, each being about five feet long and two wide. On each of these a worshipper can stand, and go through his devotions. He rises and kneels and prostrates himself, reciting his own prayers, without taking any notice of the bystanders, absorbed in worship. In the centre of the wall, under the highest dome, is the sacred niche called the *kibla*, showing the direction of Mecca. Towards this niche all the worshippers face, so as to direct their prayers towards the sacred city. This is the only necessary part of a mosque. It need have neither roof nor walls, but there must be the *kibla* indicating the true direction of Mecca. At each corner of the building there is a minaret, made of red sandstone and white marble in alternate vertical stripes, from the top of which the *muezzin* calls to prayers. These minarets are 140 feet high, and the view from the top over the city and fort and surrounding country is well worth seeing. Altogether the mosque is one of the handsomest and largest in India, and its tall minarets and white domes are a principal feature of every view of Delhi.

All round the present city of Delhi there lie the ruins of former cities, the sites of which have been occupied by successive dynasties and deserted by their successors. General Cunningham says that "the whole area covered with ruins is not less than forty-five square miles." Thus many excursions may be made to the different tombs, and mosques, and forts, which lie all round modern Delhi. There is one of these excursions which most travellers make, that to the Kutub Minar, and the ruins which surround it. These are situated eleven miles from Delhi, and all along the road there were mounds, and ruins, and tombs. The road lay through a well cultivated plain. The crops seemed ripe for harvest. In some places the oxen were treading out the corn, but in the majority of cases the beasts, which thus threshed the grain, were muzzled, contrary to the Mosaic precept. When we were still at a considerable distance from our goal, we saw the tall shaft of the Minar, tapering upwards, and as we drew nearer, we got some idea of its immense height. It is said to be the tallest column in the world, but its beauty consists rather in its proportion and adornment than in its height. It is built of red sandstone and marble, its surface is deeply fluted, and it is ornamented by bands of sculptured inscriptions in Arabic letters. The whole height is about 240 feet, and the diameter diminishes gradually. This gives the tower a very slender and graceful appearance. The surface is broken by five balconies, each richly carved, and from each of these a wonderful view is obtained over the surrounding country. What the use of this lofty tower was, is a matter of discussion. The most probable purpose for which it was built was as a tower of victory, commemorating the overthrow of the last Hindu Raja of Delhi. It may also have been used as a muezzin's tower, but its original purpose must have been something greater than that. The whole of the surrounding area was full of architectural interest. There was a mosque built out of the spoils of 27 Hindu temples, and on the carved pillars could still be traced the figures of gods and animals much defaced by the iconoclastic Mohammedans. This mosque is entered through seven gigantic arches, covered with delicate diaper patterns engraved on the stone surface. The conquered Hindus were made to use their art for their new rulers, and thus we see a combination of Mohammedan architecture covered with Hindu designs. One of the adjacent gateways is so richly carved that General Cunningham calls it "the most beautiful specimen of Pathán architecture that I have seen." There are a number of other buildings which it would be wearisome to describe in detail, but the effect of these great masses of stonework and marble, all richly carved, gave one larger ideas of the art and architecture of that early dynasty. Most of these buildings were built at the end of the 12th and the beginning of the 13th centuries by the kings of the Slave Dynasty.

Delhi is the place where the Cambridge Mission has established itself, and some account of their work may be interesting. They are by no means the first Christian workers in that city. In 1857 there was a hopeful and promising work going on, an impression being made on converts in high positions, and a flourishing school of 120 boys. Then came the Mutiny and the whole work was apparently destroyed, the missionaries were massacred, and few of the native Christians escaped. It was a heavy blow, but the work has now been reorganized. The Church of S. Stephen, so named "in memory of our fallen brethren," was opened in 1868, and is now well filled. The whole city is divided into districts, there are seven primary schools, street preaching is adopted as an effective way of stating Christian truths, and there is a large and important work being done by English ladies who visit the Zenanas. But the great accession to the work took place in 1877, when Cambridge resolved to send out some of the best educated of her sons to endeavour to reach the more thoughtful heathen. It was felt that in a large and important city like Delhi, full of keen-brained and intellectual natives, it needed well-equipped missionaries to represent the truth of Christianity. So for the last five years men of high attainments, who have won a front rank in University contests, well trained in secular learning as well as full of Christian heroism, have lived and worked in Delhi. Their chief object is high-class education, and latterly they have found an opportunity of enlarging their work. There used to be a Delhi College, which failed, and Government offered the Mission a grant-in-aid if they would undertake the work. Thus the whole of the higher education of the district is in their hands, they have a high school for boys, the first class of which is prepared for matriculation, and those who desire to complete their education are further prepared for University degrees. There are four Universities in India, viz.: Calcutta, Madras, Bombay, and Lahore. They are merely examining bodies, and confer degrees. Students are prepared at the various colleges affiliated to these Universities, of which there are 82 scattered throughout India. It may be worth while noticing that throughout India the majority of students are contented with passing the matriculation examination, and but few strive to reach the standards of F.A. (or First Arts), B.A., or M.A. This may arise from the fact that the certificate of having passed the matriculation examination is sufficient qualification for most Government offices, and few have either leisure or desire to work up to the higher degrees. In the ten years ending 1877–8, out of a total for all India of

18,610 matriculated candidates, only 1665 obtained a B.A. degree, while 296 was the total number who reached the degree of M.A. One of the members of the Cambridge Mission kindly allowed me to accompany him to their college. It is called S. Stephen's College, and is a large building with several classrooms, and a lending library well furnished with books. We arrived in time for the opening exercises, which are so arranged as to edify students of all creeds. All the classes gathered together in the central quadrangle, and a passage was read in Urdu translated from the Book of Proverbs in praise of wisdom, and then a prayer (also in Urdu) was said that wisdom might be found, and the work prosper. The prayer was offered in the name of Christ, though the number of Christian boys is at present small. Throughout the school religious teaching is given, Bible facts are taught, and lectures delivered drawing comparisons between different religions. At present the Hindu boys still worship at the idol shrines, and the new learning has not sapped the old idolatry. But it is early times yet to look for any great results, though already some scholars of high attainments have been baptized. The college which is affiliated to the Lahore University is likely to be very popular, as the teachers are men of high University standing, and they give much of their time to teaching. Their pupils seemed well cared for, the discipline was admirable, and the native pundits, who took the lower classes, were in some cases Christians. It is one of the greatest experiments yet made in India of high-class teaching on a distinctively Christian basis, carried on by men whose attainments are well authenticated. It has been sometimes made a matter of reproach that the missionaries sent out to convert the heathen have been men of small education and totally unfit to cope with Eastern philosophers. There is a certain amount of truth in this contention, though it is possible to overestimate the cleverness and subtilty of the Indian mind. No doubt a poorly educated missionary, however useful amongst savages or fetish worshippers, would do but little good amongst the philosophical Hindus. But these are not so alarming as we are sometimes inclined to imagine. Their minds are quick but superficial, very absorbent of knowledge, but not inclined to originate. And the well-trained Western mind with its slower but surer powers is more than a match for the cleverest and quickest brained Hindu. Certainly the members of the Cambridge Mission do not lie open to the reproach of being unfit to cope with any of the natives. They are men who could have made their mark at home, who were good scholars, fellows of their colleges, educated in all the wisdom of the West. These have been willing to renounce the easier career open to them at home, and have devoted their great gifts to the training and evangelizing of the inhabitants of Delhi. That city presents now but a faint reflection of its past glories, and the ruins of bygone dynasties lie thick on every side. But amongst these memorials of the past there is rising an edifice which may endure for ever. Delhi may henceforth be famous not only because of the Mogul Empire, the long sustained siege, and the Imperial Durbar; but also because there Christianity attacked cultivated heathenism in one of its strongest fortresses, and prevailed.

From Delhi on November 18th I went to Agra. This town is specially connected with the name of the Emperor Akbar, who reigned from 1556 to 1605. He was the greatest of the Mogul Emperors, his rule was the most extensive, and his policy the wisest. He did all he could to ingratiate himself with his Hindu subjects, and he employed them as administrators and officials under himself. He was by no means a strict Mohammedan, and he offended many of his co-religionists by the willingness with which he listened to the preachers of other creeds. This toleration led him at last to promulgate a new faith, "based upon natural theology, and comprising the best practices of all known creeds."* How far he was sincere it is difficult to say. The fact of his reigning over subjects of various faiths, all of whom he desired to conciliate, probably made him tolerant from motives of policy as well as from conviction. Certainly the effect of his toleration was to organize his conquests into an Empire, and both Hindus and Mohammedans were treated with an equal impartiality. His revenue system was based on ancient Hindu customs, and was similar to that at present employed by the British Government. It chiefly consisted in a land cess, the produce of each acre being valued, and one-third of the gross produce (or an equivalent money payment) being claimed by Akbar's officers. This is a larger proportion than is now exacted by us, but the custom of taxing the cultivator of the soil is the foundation of our revenue system. All through India the Government is considered to be the owner of the soil, and the land tax is in the nature of a rent-charge paid to the State. During his reign Agra was the capital of the Empire, and he built the great fort which still stands on the right bank of the Jumna, and within which was his palace and extensive quarters occupied by his numerous wives.

I visited this fort and was astonished with the magnificence and splendour of the old Imperial Palace. Much of the interior is now occupied by the arsenal, and barracks. Cannon stand in rows, and there is every appurtenance of modern warfare within the ancient walls. One of the most touching sights is a tomb surrounded by low railings, which stands in the middle of the court-yard. It is the last resting place of John Russell Colvin, the Lieutenant-Governor of the North-West Provinces at the time of the Mutiny. He and a few officers and their wives, with a few faithful soldiers, were closely be-

* W. W. Hunter's *Indian Empire*, p. 239.

sieged by the rebels in the terrible summer of 1857. Here he succumbed under the weight of care and sickness; there was no possibility of laying his body in consecrated ground, for the church and cemetery were in the hands of the mutineers. So he was laid in the midst of the fort where he died, and the tomb still stands amidst parked cannon and piles of round shot, a memorial of the time when a few brave men saved Agra from being entirely occupied by rebels. But the great interest of the fort lies in the marble palaces of the Emperor Akbar. One passes through hall after hall, and court after court, each richly inlaid with patterns of various colours and bright with precious stones. "The pavilions overhanging the river are inlaid, within and without, in the rich style of Florentine mosaic. They are precious caskets of marble, glittering all over with jasper, and agate, cornelian, bloodstone and lapis-lazuli, and topped with golden domes. Balustrades of marble, wrought in open patterns of such rich design that they resemble fringes of lace when seen from below, extend along the edge of the battlements." * Besides these there are baths, the walls of which are adorned with thousands of small mirrors, disposed in intricate designs, so that every splash of the fountain was reflected innumerable times, and the light of lamps was flashed back from every part of the surface. Within the women's quarters there is a garden, still full of roses, with fountains and vines. There are also curious underground passages, which led into the houses occupied by Akbar's numerous wives, and at the end of one passage there was once a deep well, now bricked up, down which the unfaithful ones are said to have been thrown. It is impossible to describe the richness of the marble courts, incrusted with gold, and inlaid with precious stones. It only remains to say that the *Moti Musjid*, or Pearl Mosque,

* Bayard Taylor.

within the walls of the fort, is said by Fergusson to be by far the most elegant mosque of this age, perhaps indeed of any period of Moslem art. The white marble court-yard, with its stainless domes and perfect proportions, must be seen to be appreciated.

But it is not only in the fort at Agra that one sees the perfection of Mohammedan art. Take a hired *gharri*, and drive over the bridge of boats to the Tomb of Itmad-ud-Dowlah. One gets out at a gateway which gives one admittance into a beautiful garden. In the midst of the garden rises a white marble building, surmounted by a canopy made of pierced lattice work, also of marble. As the sun shines through the patterns of this pavilion, it looks like the most delicate lace work, and is as pure and perfect as when it was first finished. This tomb was raised in 1628 by the wife of the Emperor Jehanghir, in memory of her father, who was a Persian adventurer, and noted for taking bribes. Yet he rests in one of the fairest sepulchres ever built.

It still remains to notice the greatest wonder of Agra, perhaps one of the most splendid buildings in the world, the Taj Mahál. This is a tomb erected by the Emperor Shah Jehan, in memory of his wife; he himself is also buried there, and no finer mausoleum was ever designed as this last resting place of man and wife. It is built on the banks of the Jumna, some two miles from the fort, and is enclosed in a beautiful garden within a high wall. One enters by a lofty gateway of sandstone and marble, and then looks down an avenue of dark cypress trees to where the marble domes tower upwards into the blue vault of heaven. The main idea of the structure is an octagonal building covered by a high central dome, surrounded by four smaller ones. This building stands on a terrace of white marble, with a tall and graceful minaret at each corner. There is a mosque on each side of the terrace, the front of the Taj looks down the central path of the garden towards the principal gateway, and the back of the terrace overhangs the river. But the chief wonder is the apparent unsubstantiality and fairiness of the central structure. Looking at it from the top of the gateway down the vista of dark cypress trees, the effect was like that of a scene on the stage. It seemed impossible to localize the building. One could not tell how near or how far off it really was. It seemed to recede or approach as one's fancy suggested. It sounds absurd thus to talk of a massive structure over 200 feet high. Yet I think all who have seen the Taj have been struck with this curious effect. An eminent architect told me that the effect was produced by the builder having taken care to kill all shadows. Consequently there was nothing by which one could determine the exact spot on which it rested, and thus the distant view was fairylike, unsubstantial, spectacular, scenic. From the gateway the pathway leads by marble tanks of water, which reflect the glories of the building, and as one approached nearer the wonder deepened. For one then saw how rich the details were, how the marble was everywhere inlaid with precious stones and carved in patterns, and yet the taste was so exquisite that the majesty of the main design was not spoilt by over elaboration of the separate parts. Then the inside had to be penetrated. On the basement were the real tombs of Shah Jehan and his beloved wife, which are reached by a sloping passage worn smooth by the feet of thousands. Her tomb is in the centre, and his by her side, contrary to the usual custom of Mohammedan rulers, who generally claimed the chief place for themselves. Above on the main floor, under the central dome, inside an octagon screen carved in lace work patterns, there were the cenotaphs. The echo from the dome seemed to me purer and far superior to that in the Baptistery at Pisa, for when the four notes of a chord were sung they came back mingled in perfect harmony, and the sound lingered long, and at last died away in exquisite softness. All round the central building there is a marble terrace, so that a clear view can be obtained from all sides. It took a long time to see the whole, for the view from the adjacent minaret was well worth seeing, and the neighbouring mosques had to be visited. It is altogether a perfect place. One cannot criticize or object to a single detail, one could not imagine any improvement or suggest any alteration. No corpse rests in a fairer sepulchre. I visited it once by moonlight; the gardens were nearly deserted, and the dim white light added to the charm of the marble walls and swelling domes. Within all was dark save one dim oil lamp burning over the tombs. The stillness was unbroken by any voice, only the ceaseless chirp of the crickets made the absence of other noises the more noticeable. It was the quietest, most peaceful resting-place possible, and the beauty and charm of the whole structure were perfect. There is, I think, no building in Europe which can be compared with the Taj. It surpasses all both in grandeur and symmetry of design and perfect beauty of detail.

Every visitor to Agra is bound to make an expedition to Futtehpore Sikri. This is the palace which the Emperor Akbar built, and is about 22 miles from Agra. It has been compared to Windsor, and it must have borne much the same relation to the capital, as that castle does to London. It was the country residence of the great Emperor, only such a magnificent residence as only he could have designed and built. The circuit of the walls is seven miles, and within that area there were palaces and zenanas, halls and courts, mosques and stables, pleasure-grounds and caravanserais, game preserves and hunting lodges, all that could conduce to luxury, and magnificence, and splendour. It would be wearisome if I was to try to enumerate the different buildings. I can only refer the curious to the excellent guide-book written by H. G. Keene, and mention a few of the wonders of the place. The ruins stand on a rocky hill, and the material of which they were built is a red sandstone. This stone is soft enough to be richly carved, yet the grain is so close that these carvings are still clear and sharp, where they have escaped rude and destructive hands. The most striking building within the enceinte is the great mosque, with a marble shrine built over the tomb of a Mohammedan saint, who recommended the Emperor to make Futtehpore his residence. The great gateway which overlooks the town below and is reached by a long flight of steps, is said by Fergusson to be the finest in India. On it are carved several sentences, which show the eclectic character of Akbar's religion. One is thus translated: "Said Jesus, on whom be peace! The world is a bridge, pass over it but build no house there: he who hopeth for an hour may hope for an eternity: the world is but an hour, spend it in devotion: the rest is unseen." Most of the other buildings are palaces which were built for the numerous wives of the Emperor, and public offices for the despatch of business. One of these palaces is called the house of Miriam, and is said to have been occupied by a Christian wife. It shows traces of a painting said to be a representation of the Annunciation, but too defaced to be clearly made out. The richness of the carving is noticeable in all the buildings. The walls in many of the rooms are covered all over with delicate diaper patterns cut in relief. The cornices and ceilings are also richly carved, and the whole shows a lavishness of ornament and expenditure of labour, which would now be impossible. One court-yard has squares of black and white marble laid down in the form of a *pachisi* board, on which a game something similar to backgammon was played with living pieces. From the chief palace a long covered passage extends over the roofs of other buildings, and leads down into the caravanserai; it was used by the great ladies of the Court, who were enabled by this means to see the merchants display their goods, and perhaps break the monotony of harem life by engaging in a little bargaining. All these palaces and buildings are now in ruins. The city only had a life of 50 years, as soon after Akbar's death it was deserted. When it was inhabited, it must have seen a wonderful Court life, and its remains tell us something of the greatness of this Solomon of the East.

After seeing Futtehpore Sikri, it is well to go to Sekundra, where Akbar was buried. The mausoleum is about six miles from Agra, and stands in a large enclosure, which has four beautiful gateways. From each of these gateways a grand causeway of hewn stone leads up to the central building, which is above 100 feet high. This is built in five stories, the four lower ones being of sandstone, while the highest is of white marble. Here on the summit of the building, there is an enclosed space, open to the sky, surrounded by battlements of white marble carved into patterns of great richness and variety, in the centre of which is the marble cenotaph. Near it is a short stone column, on which is said to have been placed the great diamond, or *kohinoor;* this was looted by the Persian invader, Nadir Shah; it was afterwards captured by Runjeet Singh, and finally came into the possession of the Queen. The real tomb of Akbar is in a dark vaulted chamber on the basement story, and here rests the greatest of the Mogul Emperors.

At Sekundra there is an interesting Christian orphanage and printing establishment, which is one of the oldest missionary institutions in the North-West. It suffered much during the Mutiny, and the machinery was broken and burnt, and the type thrown down wells. But it has revived, and is now doing an excellent work. The children are taught printing and carpentering, the cleverest are prepared for college, and some have been ordained. The printing establishment is located in an old building, said to have been the tomb of Akbar's Christian wife. If the legend is true, this building may be said to be reconsecrated by the work at present going on in it. There seems great doubt, however, as to whether the Emperor ever had a Christian or European wife. The Jesuits certainly visited his Court, and they may have induced some Portugese lady to enter his harem, in the hopes of thus winning him over to Christianity. It would have been a wonderful triumph for them if they could have converted the Great Mogul.

It has been said that if the English are ever driven out of India, the public buildings they have erected will compare very unfavourably with the marvellous architectural wonders of the Mogul Empire. Men have jokingly remarked that our chief relics would be empty soda-water bottles and hideous barracks, and that these would be the only signs of our departed greatness. How would these contrast with the Kutub Minar or the Taj Mahal? There is a certain amount of truth in this contention, but there is another side to the picture. The glories of the old Mogul Empire were confined to the palaces and tombs of the rulers; they did not extend to the subject races. The buildings are indeed beautiful, but they were erected at a grievous cost. The labour was all forced, and the distress and mortality amongst the work-people were frightful. If the buildings remain as a wonder for ever, we must not forget the mode in which they were erected. Our rule will not be marked by any such selfish expenditure undertaken solely for the glorification of one man. If we leave any relics behind us, they will tell a different tale, viz.: that the rulers cared more for the well-being of their subjects than for their own fame. Future ages may condemn us for the want of taste shown in our buildings, they will not be able to say that the natives were neglected or ill-treated. Such public works as survive will show that the largest sums were spent in improving the communications and insuring the safety of the people. We have dug canals, at the cost of millions of pounds, which save large areas from danger of famine. We have made roads and railways which open up all parts of the country. Our railway bridges, though not always beautiful as works of art, are yet triumphs of engineering skill, and when the New Zealander of the future looks at the broken girders of the enormous structures which now span the Jumna or the Ganges, he will at least confess that the rulers who erected them were not careless of the comfort of their people. It may seem absurd to compare an iron railway bridge with a pure marble mausoleum like the Taj. Yet these two works aptly express the difference between the English and the Mogul idea of Empire. The glory of the chief ruler was the most important thing in the old Empire; the comfort of the ruled is the chief object in the new. The two erections may also serve as examples of the taste of the two Empires, and while we give the palm to the building erected by the Mogul, we must not overlook the greater utility of the less ornate structure. It might be possible to combine something of beauty with an equal amount of serviceableness. Certainly the later public buildings of Bombay and Calcutta are architecturally pleasing as well as useful, and the Public Works Department (so often abused) is beginning to be alive to the necessity of showing some taste in its erections. Certainly if we have to confess that the old Mohammedan rulers surpassed us in the beauty of their residences, we may fairly claim to have improved on their ideas of government, and to have added more than they did to the comfort and well-being and prosperity of the subject race.

CHAPTER IV.

LEAVING Agra with its memorials of the Empire of the Moguls, I journeyed on to Cawnpore, which will ever be memorable for its associations with the Sepoy Mutiny in 1857. How suddenly that fearful Mutiny broke out, many still living can remember. Like a thunderclap out of a clear sky, without special warning or apparent cause, the news was suddenly flashed through India that the native soldiers at Meerut had revolted, had massacred many Europeans, and had streamed off to Delhi. Similar risings took place throughout the North-West and Oudh, the English officers belonging to the native regiments were generally shot by their own men, and in a few weeks' time nearly the whole of the Bengal army were in arms against us. It is not possible for me to write a history of the Mutiny. That has been done by practised pens. It was a time of awful anxiety, of heroic deeds, of magnificent devotion, of terrible crimes. Each episode of the rising has its own history of suffering and valour. Each station is marked by some special memory of that blood-stained summer. But amongst all the annals of massacre and terror the town of Cawnpore will ever be associated with the worst excesses and blackest atrocities perpetrated at the time. There the treacherous Nana Sahib made his name for ever infamous. He was the adopted heir of the last of the Peshwas, and thus he would have been the hereditary ruler of the Marhattás. At this time he resided at Bithoor, within a few miles of Cawnpore, and nourished a grievance against the British Government, because the pension, which the last Peshwa enjoyed, had not been continued to him. At first when news came of the revolt of the Sepoys, he professed loyalty to the

English cause; he was put in charge of the Arsenal and Treasury, and he was told all the plans made by the small English garrison for their own defence. But as soon as the troops mutinied, he put himself at their head, and raised the standard of revolt. Then the small garrison of the English was almost at his mercy. They had withdrawn from the cantonments, and with their women and children they had entrenched themselves hastily in a small camp outside the town. Here for nineteen days they endured a siege, holding the lines of their defences against overwhelming odds and suffering terrible privations. Then came offers of negotiations, and a treaty was eventually signed which was to insure the safe conduct of the little garrison down the Ganges to Allahabad. Hampered by the number of non-combatants, and short of provisions, the English commander determined to evacuate his position, which would soon have become untenable, and to trust to the promises made by the Nana. In the early morning the little band left the intrenchments, and, with the women and children in the centre, marched to the river bank, where boats had been provided for their safe conduct down the river. Then followed a treachery which seems almost incredible. While the party were embarking, a murderous fire was opened from both banks of the river, and numbers of the English were there slaughtered. Four only out of the little band managed to escape to tell the tale. The survivors, who were not shot down at the time, were marched back as prisoners into the town of Cawnpore. The men were immediately shot, the women and children were confined in a large house. Here they remained for nearly three weeks without any comforts or news from the outer world. The fancy fails to picture the condition of this remnant of the once gay society of Cawnpore, who had endured all the trials of the siege, had then been eye-witnesses of the massacre on the river side, and were now close prisoners at the mercy of a pitiless tyrant, who had shown himself as cruel as he was treacherous. Their sufferings were soon brought to an end in a manner which still thrills with horror all who hear of it. The English army under Havelock was advancing nearer and nearer to Cawnpore. The Nana knew that his reign was soon to be over. He determined to do a deed which remains without a parallel in history. He decided to murder in cold blood all these helpless prisoners. Into that house of misery executioners were sent, who literally hacked to death these unarmed and unresisting women and children. The work of slaughter went on for a considerable time, but it is better not to try to fancy what happened within those fast-shut doors. Night fell on the work completed. The Nana is said to have passed the evening with singing and dancing. In the morning orders were given to clear the house, and the bodies were dragged to a well and there cast down. It is feared that some of the poor creatures were still breathing when they were thus hurled down this deep and narrow orifice. When the English troopers rode into the city, the blood-stained floor of the house, and the well with its tangled mass of human limbs, told them the horrors which had happened, and which they were too late to avert. The Cawnpore massacre remains as an atrocity unparalleled in history, and the sufferings thus endured by our fellow-countrymen can never be forgotten.

It seemed fitting that the sites of such terrible events should be marked by some suitable memorials. In "Wheeler's Entrenchment" as it is called, there has been built the Memorial Church. This is a handsome structure of red brick, cruciform in shape, with a triforium and clerestory, and a lofty campanile. The walls are covered with memorial tablets, commemorating those who died during the Mutiny. Round the altar are to be placed white marble slabs, and on them are to be inscribed the names of all those who died at Cawnpore. The building is one of the handsomest churches in India, and it is a fitting memorial of the brave men who held the camp so well against overwhelming odds.

The "Slaughter Ghât," as it is now named, is also pointed out to visitors.

But the chief sight is the Memorial Well, and here every care has been lavished to beautify the spot where such a terrible deed was done. The ground all round the well is kept as a garden; about fifty acres have been planted with flowering shrubs, and laid out with broad gravel paths. The grass is constantly watered, and the beds of flowers and shady walks are beautifully cared for. In the centre, over the mouth of the well which was filled up and covered in, there stands a marble statue of an angel holding a palm branch in its hand. Round the pedestal is an inscription which tells how that "a great number of Christian people, chiefly women and children, were here massacred and thrown — the living with the dead — into the well beneath." Round this figure there is a gothic screen carved in stone, which incloses the spot where so many hapless people are buried. Over the door of the screen is the text, "These are they which came out of great tribulation." It is impossible to gaze unmoved at such a sad spot, thus marked by such touching words. The whole garden is kept as a sacred place. Carriages are only allowed to proceed at a foot's pace, and no games are permitted to be played therein. Natives are also entirely excluded. The time seems now to have come when this embargo might be taken off. It would be more in the spirit of the religion we profess, if forgiveness was now granted to all, and the garden thrown open to the public without any distinction of creed or colour. There would be no fear that such a permission would be abused, and the remains of the dead are not honoured by being thus fenced off from the apparent fear of contamination from the presence of natives.

It must always be remembered that the Mutiny was in no sense a popular rising or a revolt of the whole native population. If it had been, our rule in India would have probably come to an end. But it was almost entirely a military insurrection, confined to the majority of the native soldiers we had trained, and joined by a few bad characters amongst the population. But the large majority of the natives of India never participated in the rising, many of the native soldiers remained true to our cause, and the relieving armies were largely composed of natives from Madras, Bombay, and the Punjab. It therefore seems unwise to treat the whole native population of India as in any way sympathising with the atrocities perpetrated by the mutineers at Cawnpore. Yet while we forbid them to enter the Memorial Garden, we seem to accuse the whole subject-race of being sharers in the crimes wrought by a few of their nation. It is hardly fair thus to refuse a privilege to all the members of the race because some of their number, twenty-five years ago, committed atrocious crimes. The time has now surely come for forgiveness, and the loyal natives are more likely to feel horror at the crimes wrought by their countrymen, when they see that we do not look upon all as equally guilty. We should appeal to their best feelings, when they saw that we considered the Mutiny as the work of a few misguided and faithless men, and that we did not wish to condemn the whole nation because of the crimes of these few.

From Cawnpore I travelled to Lucknow, which is also famous for Mutiny reminiscences. But the town itself is interesting in many ways, and has played a part in the later history of India. It is the capital of the Province of Oudh, and is the most populous town in India next to the Presidency capitals, having 284,779 inhabitants.

The Province of Oudh, which is about half the size of England, was a part of the Mogul Empire, which was governed by a Nawáb Vizier. About 1750 the Province became practically independent of the Emperor of Delhi, and the then Vizier became a feudatory reigning Prince, and the administration became hereditary in his family. From this date we read of the "Kings of Oudh." Lucknow was made the capital of their "kingdom," and most of the public buildings were built at the end of the last and the beginning of the present century. Under the Governor-Generalships of Clive and Warren Hastings the Nawábs of Oudh were generally friendly to the British, and their dominions were therefore not taken from them, though they were forced to pay large sums to the East Indian Company. Their political position being thus assured, "the rulers of Oudh turned their attention to cock fighting and beast fighting; to fireworks, dancing girls and champagne; and they spent the money, in the enjoyment of which their powerful protectors guaranteed them, in building seraglios and in furnishing them with lustres and mirrors, with glass lions and porcelain negroes." *

The later history of the Province is one long story of misrule and dissolute living, varied by threats from the British Resident of annexation. The administration of Oudh was disgraceful and the inhabitants were groaning under the most evil government which existed in India. Threats and warnings had no effect in improving the state of the Province, and at last Lord Dalhousie in 1856 determined to annex the whole of the King's dominions. This decision has been questioned, and some have traced the cause of the Mutiny (which broke out in the following year) to Lord Dalhousie's policy. They have said that he roused the feelings of the natives against our rule, and that they thought the annnexation of Oudh unjust, as the independence of the King had been guaranteed by treaty. Certainly Lord Dalhousie never doubted the justice of his policy. He was guided entirely by his desire to do his duty to the inhabitants of Oudh. By a treaty made in 1837 the King of Oudh had been warned that systematic oppression would lead to deposition. The

* Keene's *Guide to Lucknow*, p. 69.

condition of the country had become worse since then. And at last Lord Dalhousie ordered General (afterwards Sir James) Outram to assume the direct administration of Oudh, on the ground that "the British Government would be guilty in the sight of God and man if it were any longer to aid in sustaining by its countenance an administration fraught with suffering to millions." The decree went forth, the King was deposed, and he now lives as a State pensioner in a suburb of Calcutta. Oudh was annexed to the British dominions, and two millions of suffering people must bless the day when they passed under our just rule.

The chief buildings of Lucknow are the palaces, and seraglios, and hunting lodges, on which the Kings of Oudh wasted the resources of the Province. These are vulgar and poor in design, chiefly made of brick, covered with stucco, and mean in their details. Their only beauty consists in their sky lines, which are sometimes quaint, and not without a certain originality and grace. The most fantastic of these is the Chatta Manzal, so called from its being topped with a gilt umbrella (*chatta*). It used to be one of the seraglios of the King, but it is now used as a club house and library by the European residents. Though the materials of which it is made are only brick and stucco, yet its quaint pinnacles and buttresses render it a very original structure, not without architectural beauty.

The largest of the palaces is the Imambara, which was built in 1784. It is said to have been a famine-relief work, on which multitudes of the people were glad to labour, the wages being paid at night time so that none might know who had been forced by want to apply for work. This great palace is built round a large quadrangle one side of which is taken up by a great hall 162 feet long and 53 feet wide. This immense building is roofed over by a coarse concrete several feet in thickness. This was originally laid on a rude mould of brick, but when it was thoroughly set and dry the mould was removed and the vaulting remained, covering the entire building. This great hall is at present used as an arsenal, where quantities of cannon are stored. On another side of the court-yard there stands a mosque, which is at present not used for worship. The whole of this palace is garrisoned by English soldiers, and has been converted into a strong fort. There is a talk of razing the fortifications, and restoring the palace to the Mohammedans, so that they may once more use their mosque. I believe the fort is not strategically useful, as it can be commanded from other heights. We have held it ever since the Mutiny. It seems hard that the Mohammedans should be debarred from worshipping in one of the most famous mosques in Lucknow, and if the fortifications do not add to the strength of the English defences, it would be wiser to restore the place to the inhabitants of the city.

The chief interest, however, of Lucknow does not lie in the palaces and stuccoed abominations of the Kings of Oudh. They were as poor architects as they were bad rulers. But the main sights of the place are connected with the gallant defence made by Sir Henry Lawrence in 1857, and the relief brought to the little garrison by Havelock and Outram. Every visitor to Lucknow visits the ruins of the Residency, where a small British force resisted for eighty-seven days an army of rebels. Surrounded by foes, having to watch day and night against surprises and attacks, hampered by the presence of women and children, cannonaded by artillery, and attacked by mines, less than 1000 Europeans and 500 faithful natives held out against 100,000 assailants.

"Men will forget what we suffer and not what we do. We can fight—
But to be soldier all day and be sentinel all thro' the night—
Ever the mine and assault, our sallies, their lying alarms.
Bugles and drums in the darkness, and shoutings and soundings to arms,
Ever the labour of fifty that had to be done by five,

Ever the marvel among us that one should be left alive,
Ever the day with its traitorous death from the loopholes around,
Ever the night with its coffinless corpse to be laid in the ground,
Heat like the mouth of a hell, or a deluge of cataract skies,
Stench of old offal decaying, and infinite torment of flies,
Thoughts of the breezes of May blowing over an English field,
Cholera, scurvy, and fever, the wound that *would* not be heal'd,
Lopping away of the limb by the pitiful—pitiless knife,—
Torture and trouble in vain,—for it never could save us a life.
Valour of delicate women who tended the hospital bed,
Horror of women in travail among the dying and dead,
Grief for our perishing children, and never a moment for grief,
Toil and ineffable weariness, faltering hopes of relief,
Havelock baffled, or beaten, or butcher'd for all that we knew—
Then day and night, day and night, coming down on the still-shattered walls
Millions of musket-bullets, and thousands of cannon balls—
But ever upon the topmost roof our banner of England blew."

So our great poet describes the terrors of that fierce siege. Sir Henry Lawrence was wounded and died on the third day of the investment. But he had victualled and fortified the palace as far as it was possible, and it was owing to his foresight and careful preparations that the defenders were able to hold out for such a length of time.

The ruins of the Residency remain in the same condition as it was left by the mutineers. The ground all round has been levelled and laid out as a garden, and within the precincts rise the ruins of the Residency. It was built at the end of the last century, and was a large and commodious house, and attached to it there were other smaller houses, together with a small church and graveyard. The whole was enclosed by a wall, but it is now difficult to trace all the different buildings. The walls are scarred by shot and shell, the rooms are all unroofed, and the whole place is a ruin. For after it was evacuated by Havelock's relieving force it was occupied by the mutineers, who blew up certain portions, and were not driven out till the final advance of our troops in March, 1858. But there is still one staircase left standing, which leads up to the watch tower from which "the banner of

England flew" all through those hot months, when the women and children were hidden in the cellars, when there was no water for washing (a terrible privation in such a climate), and when the hospital was as much under fire as the house itself. The hole in the wall which the shell made which killed Sir Henry Lawrence, and the remains of the room in which he died, are still visible. Close by is the cemetery where numbers are buried who died during the long siege. Many of the inscriptions are in memory of women and little children, and are touching in their simplicity. But the simplest and most touching inscription of all is cut on the plain stone slab, which tells that

"Here lies Henry Lawrence, who tried to do his duty."

For a long time there was no memorial of those native soldiers who remained faithful to us in spite of threats, and bribes, and every kind of temptation. But Lord Northbrook during his viceroyalty out of his own private purse put up a stone to their honour.

While I was at Lucknow the whole place was *en fête*, for the Viceroy was to hold a great Durbar, which was to be attended by all the Talukdars of Oudh. The coming of the Viceroy to a place is no light matter, for his retinue is so enormous that no building could contain the numbers who travel with him. So outside the city, on a bare and open piece of ground, there were arranged a number of tents of all shapes and sizes, enough to form a small town. This was the Viceregal Camp, and was a marvel of canvas-building. In the centre was the great Durbar tent, of bright coloured yellow walls, spread with costly carpets, and capable of holding several hundred people. Opening from that there were other tents, used as dining or drawing rooms, bedrooms, &c., all of which together made quarters for the Viceroy and his suite. In front of these tents there was a large circular plot of the greenest turf, with a great flagstaff in the centre, and all round this central space there stretched streets of tents in every direction, which were occupied by members of the Government, aides-de-camp, civilians, officers, and officials of all sorts. Near to this canvas town there were pitched other camps, occupied by various regiments both of horse and foot, for as a great review was to be held, the place was full of troops. All this magnificent array had sprung up in the midst of a bare and sandy plain. The very turf had been specially laid down for the occasion, a special telegraph wire had been brought to the camp, and the various resident officials had been busy for weeks before, preparing for the Viceroy's visit. He was to remain at Lucknow altogether for six days, and when he left, all the tents would be struck and the troops would depart, and the spot return to its original loneliness.

However, for that week every one was in a state of excitement, and I was glad to have an opportunity of getting a glimpse of the show. The Viceroy arrived on a Saturday, but the entry into the town was made in private, in consequence of a death having lately occurred in Lady Ripon's family. Sunday was spent in quietness, though as the Churches could not accommodate all the troops then collected in Lucknow, I was asked to take a camp-service for one regiment. This I was glad to do, and had a very attentive congregation, who formed a hollow square, a pile of drums forming the reading desk, and hymns being sung to the accompaniment of the military band. On Monday the Viceregal party made expeditions, and transacted business, and in the evening there was a dinner party, followed by a levée. This was held in the largest tent, and here a long string of the European residents of the place passed before the Viceroy and made their bow. Tuesday there was a review of all the troops in the station, and the presentation of new colours to one of the native regiments. This was a very brilliant sight, as the Indian regiments have bright coloured uniforms of red, and green, and gold, and their turbans look picturesque. One of the English regiments had only just landed from Egypt, and the uniforms of the men looked stained and weather-worn. In the evening the Lieutenant-Governor gave a ball in the club-rooms at the Chatta Manzal. I never saw a gayer sight. The different uniforms lightened up the sombreness of the usual evening attire of the gentlemen, and the rooms were large, well lighted, and beautifully decorated. There was an open air rendezvous on some steps leading down to the river, which was illuminated by Chinese lanterns and was gay with flowers in pots, and here one could escape from the heat of the ball-room into the cloudless glories of an Indian night. But the great event of the week was on Wednesday, when the Viceroy held his Durbar, or levée for native nobility and their retainers. The big tents were thrown into one, a throne was set at one end, and a broad central pathway was laid down with scarlet cloth. The Europeans sat on one side, and the natives on the other, and all had to be in their places before the Viceroy arrived. He drove up punctually at 12 o'clock under a salute of twenty-one guns, the troops outside presented arms, the band played "God save the Queen," everyone in the tent stood up, and then there passed up the centre the little knot of men who were the chief rulers of this part of India. Last of all came the Viceroy, dressed in Court dress, wearing the Garter ribbon, and the Grand Cross of the Star of India. It was a most variegated and brilliant sight to see this great tent full of people, the uniforms and ladies' dresses filling up one side, while opposite there were the natives, clothed in velvet and satin garments, bright with gold brocade, and with turbans heavy with jewels. When the Viceroy had entered and taken his seat on the throne, the natives (in number about 200) were led up in order and presented. Their rank seemed very strictly defined, and the order of precedence rigidly adhered to. Some of the representatives of the oldest families were quite young children, who had just succeeded to their estates. As each was presented, he offered a gold coin in token of fealty, which the Viceroy touched, and then it was retained by the owner. When all had been presented, there was an address to the Viceroy, read by one of the chief nobles. He spoke of the loyalty they felt for the Crown, and thanked the present Viceroy for the interest he had shown in the natives of India, notably by the measures lately introduced for local self-government, and the appointment of the commission on education. The Viceroy read a speech in answer. In it he referred to Sir H. Lawrence, and the epitaph on his tomb, and said how he would try to imitate a man so connected with Oudh. He also gave them some advice about attending to the needs of their tenants, and praised the Chief Commissioner of Oudh, and told them to ask his advice in any difficulty. After he had finished his speech, the Foreign Secretary read it out again in Urdu, so that those ignorant of English might know what had been said. Then betel nut and pán were handed round, and the proceedings closed, the Viceroy leaving with salutes, and music, and military parade.

There seemed to be a curious difficulty as to how the natives were to show their respect. The old way was for a native to take off his shoes when he came into a room, as he could not remove his turban without disgrace. But as Western ideas have spread, the richer natives no longer wear Indian shoes, which are easily slipped off, but wear English patent leather boots. How then is the native to show respect? He cannot easily slip off his English boots, and it would be a disgrace to him to uncover his head. Apparently the difficulty is not solved, and the custom seems to be that when a man wears native shoes he takes them off, while if he has on English-made boots, he need not remove them. Certainly all the natives at the Durbar wore English shoes or boots, which they did not remove, and thus showed no outward sign of respect, but walked up the central passage over the scarlet cloth with both head and feet covered. As an Englishman always removes his hat, there seems something of an inequality, but it is one of those abstruse points only to be properly decided by a Court Chamberlain or other State Master of the Ceremonies. The ignorant unofficial person cannot hope to penetrate such mysteries.

On the same afternoon the Viceroy distributed the prizes at the Martinière College. This college was founded by a French adventurer named Claude Martine, who after serving under the Frenchman Lally in Southern India, and afterwards in the Company's army, finally took service under the King of Oudh, and died at Lucknow in the year 1800. He left behind him a large fortune, most of which was bequeathed to the three cities of Calcutta, Lucknow, and Lyons, for the foundation of schools in each. The school at Lucknow is accommodated in a great palace which Martine built, and in the basement of which his body is buried. It is said that he decided on this curious arrangement for fear of the King of Oudh frustrating his charitable intentions, and seizing on his palace. For Martine rightly judged that though an Eastern ruler might not respect the testamentary wishes of a dead man, yet he would hardly violate the sanctity of a tomb. So by ordering that his body should be placed within the walls of his house, he insured that the building should not be confiscated by any rapacious ruler. The structure itself is noted as one of the strangest and most fantastic even amongst the bizarre and quaint erections which abound in Lucknow. Greek orders are superimposed one upon another, the sky line is broken by numberless statues, flying buttresses uphold a central tower crowned by a belvedere and a flagstaff, and figures of lions "stand erect holding on to the battlements with one paw while they gesticulate oratorically with the other; all this makes up an *ensemble* which is certainly unique and may even be called striking." *

The school, which is located in this curious building, gives a good education to English and Eurasian boys and girls. The boys work for the matriculation examination at the Calcutta University, and also strive to enter the Roorki Engineering College. This latter opening has lately been in some measure closed against them, as a new resolution passed by Government gives the preference to the employment of native engineers rather than Europeans. There are only a few Government posts offered for competition, and these are now almost entirely restricted to natives. Those interested in Eurasian schools feel hurt by this new resolution, and desire that the appointments should be offered for open competition irrespective of race. The point was brought forward by the Principal of the Martinière College in his opening address to the Viceroy, but Lord Ripon in his reply naturally refrained from touching on such debatable points. He contented himself with saying a few pleasant words to the prizewinners, who came up to receive the books and other rewards which they had gained. He departed amidst hearty cheers from the boys, and without further allusion to these burning questions. There are so few openings in India for Eurasian boys, and they are so liable to become worthless if left uneducated, that it is no wonder that all who are interested in their future watch very jealously any curtailment of the offices to which they might be appointed. Still the spread of railway works and the increase of manufactures open out careers for them as overseers and supervisors of native workmen, and their mixed blood enables them to stand the climate better than the pure European. In every way the Eurasian is now being looked after, and if he has any good qualities in him, he ought never to sink into the

* Keene's *Guide to Lucknow*.

position of the "poor white trash" known in the American States.

In the evening of the same day the Viceroy gave an evening party at his Camp, to which both natives and English were invited. The big tent was full of ladies in bright dresses, officers in uniform, and natives in gorgeous clothes and jewelled turbans. The Viceroy with his A.D.C. moved about amongst his guests, and had a word with the chief nobles and other persons who were introduced to him.

The Talukdars of Oudh are the territorial magnates of that Province. They are responsible to the Government for a gross sum payable from their lands, and occupy nearly the position of great English landlords. Previous to the Mutiny they were an uneducated and dissolute class, but the younger generation bear a better character. Canning College has been founded in Lucknow for their education, and the majority of the younger nobles can speak English. Some appeared over fat and unhealthy in appearance, but others had bright intelligent faces. These Talukdars gave a grand open air evening *fête* in honour of the Viceroy's visit on the next day to that on which the Durbar was held, in the Kaiser Bagh. This is a great enclosed garden surrounded by rooms originally built as a seraglio, but now used as a caravanserai by the nobles when they come into Lucknow. The whole court-yard was illuminated with countless oil lamps, arranged in various devices, there was a great display of fireworks, and as the night was still and dark the effect was striking.

This closed the festivities of the week. The Viceroy proceeded on his way to Calcutta, the great Camp was struck, and Lucknow no doubt soon relapsed into its usual quiet state. But the good effect of such visits it is hard to over estimate. They give the Viceroy an insight into various parts of India, they bring him into contact with the notable people of each district, and he can see with his own eyes and hear with his own ears what is being done. People in England forget the enormous size and the various races which make up what we call India. The territory over which the Viceroy rules is as large as all Europe without Russia. The different races differ amongst themselves as much as Frenchmen and Germans, Spaniards and Englishmen. The conditions of life vary in different parts; the soil, the requirements, the civilization, the manners and customs alter in every province. No one could legislate for the whole, if he only had knowledge of a part. What would be useful for one place might be undesirable in another. Therefore the more the ruler of such an Empire can visit different parts, the more likely he is to gain experience and avoid mistakes. The commonest time of the year for such visits is during the month of November, while the Government is making its periodical move from Simla to Calcutta. All the hot weather it remains in the hills, and from November to March it is located in Calcutta. The distance between the two places is over 1100 miles (about the distance between London and Gibraltar), and the time taken in transferring the paraphernalia of government from one place to another is considerable. During this interval the Viceroy takes the opportunity of visiting some new portion of the Empire, and becoming personally acquainted with its needs and requirements. He often holds a *levée* for the chief inhabitants of the district, and thus can interchange opinions with the residents on the spot. Thus he can gain experience and see how different parts of the extensive dominions which he has to govern are progressing.

It would take too much space to describe the whole scheme of the government of India, but it may be advisable to state a few facts for the use of those who are very ignorant of the subject. Before 1858 the Governor-General was almost an autocrat, responsible only to a distant Court of Directors in England, and often forced to act before he could receive either advice or orders from home. In 1858 the

Crown assumed the direct government of India, the Governor-General was changed into a Viceroy, and all his acts have now to be sanctioned by a Secretary of State in England, who is a Cabinet Minister. This Secretary of State is assisted by a Council, chiefly composed of retired Indian officials, who advise him on all questions which are referred home for decision. Thus the Viceroy in India is not supreme, but all his actions are controlled by a responsible Minister in England. This sometimes leads to delay, and is likely also to hamper at times the policy of the Government in India. It might possibly happen that through a change of parties at home, the Viceroy might find himself no longer able to work in harmony with the Secretary of State. (This indeed happened in 1880, when Lord Lytton resigned simultaneously with the home Government.) But usually matters work smoothly. India remains outside the sphere of party politics at home, and the reference of all questions to a responsible Minister in England prevents hasty legislation, and brings outside public opinion to bear on Indian affairs. This is a good thing in the main, as if India were governed by an irresponsible clique of officials, however excellent, they would be liable to be warped by prejudices, and might fail to reform abuses. Irresponsible power is good for no man, and though often it is necessary to refer many small matters home for sanction, yet the constant check thus placed on legislation and expenditure gives time for thought and prevents extravagance. It is said in India that the Viceroy could not appoint an extra servant without sanction from home, and though this is perhaps an exaggeration, yet the careful enquiry into every item of expenditure must act beneficially.

In India the government is carried on as follows: In grave cases of emergency the Viceroy can act independently, but usually he governs through his Council. This Council is twofold. First there is the

Executive Council, consisting of about six official members, which may be compared to the Cabinet at home. Each member of this Council is head of a department, and in this way there are bureaux or portfolios of Foreign Affairs, Finance, Home, War, Law, and Public Works. And next there is the Legislative Council, made up of the members of the Executive Council, "with the addition of the Governor of the Province in which it may be held, and official delegates from Madras and Bombay, together with certain nominated members representative of the non-official native and European communities." * This Council meets when required, its debates are public, and it discusses bills and passes measures, which eventually become laws. The debates are said to lack interest. The members often read their speeches, and these state papers, though very valuable, sound dull when compared with the freer parliamentary discussion which takes place at home. Yet a seat in the Council is highly prized, the men who fill these posts are the wisest officials in India, and the amount of work done in each Department is enormous. The table of a Member of Council is covered with papers, boxes full of weighty matters requiring his decision surround his chair, and his office has to provide information on all points connected with the Department he represents.

Besides this supreme Council there are also provincial legislative Councils for the Presidencies of Bombay and Madras, and for the Lieutenant-Governorship of Bengal. The members of these Councils confer on local and provincial matters, and though they cannot legislate independently of the Viceroy, they have large powers in domestic and administrative matters.

British India is divided into twelve Provinces, the best known of which are Madras, Bombay, Bengal, the Punjab, the North-West Provinces, Burma, and

* W. W. Hunter's *Indian Empire*, p. 329.

Assam. Bombay and Madras are ruled over by a Governor appointed direct from England, and though they are subject to the supreme power of the Viceroy, he seldom interferes with their internal actions. The other Provinces are ruled over by a covenanted civilian, who has won his way upwards from the lowest grade of his profession. He is called either the Lieutenant-Governor or the Chief Commissioner, according to the Province over which he rules. Some of these Provinces are over 100,000 square miles in area, and over these large tracts of country full of people the English civilian practically reigns supreme. All executive power rests in his hands, and the well-being of millions of people is entrusted to him.

Under him there are several district officers who are responsible for the good order of their districts. The whole of our territory in India is divided into these districts, which vary in size and in population, and are about 240 in number. An average district would be about 60 miles square and would contain about 800,000 people. They might be compared to the larger counties of England. The chief officer of such a district is called a Collector-Magistrate, or a Deputy-Commissioner. It would be impossible to enumerate the variety of work which is expected from a District Officer. He is both a revenue officer, and also a magistrate and judge with large powers. He has to concern himself about police and jails, roads and sanitary matters, schools and dispensaries. A great part of the cold weather is spent by him in travelling about his district. His tents are pitched wherever his presence seems desirable, and thus all parts of his charge are visited in turn. Justice is thus brought to the doors of the poor, abuses are enquired into, quarrels arranged, and disputes adjudicated on the spot. There is no village so remote, but it is liable to be visited by the chief official of the district, and this constant supervision insures due care in all his subordinates.

The career of an Indian civilian is one of the most interesting which can be conceived. He has work enough to satisfy the most gluttonous, he is always engaged in improving the material well-being of his fellow-subjects, and he has scope for all his talents and ability. The work is hard and often distressing, but the training which a young man receives is such as to call out all the good which is in him, and to fit him to govern others. The life in the districts is often lonely, the climate in the hot weather is most trying, and the work at times becomes monotonous. But promotion is always expected, and each member of the Civil Service can leave his mark on the district in which he works. English people hardly realize the excellence of the administration which is daily carried on in India by the civilians. Yet the ability, and industry, and rectitude of principle, and doggedness of purpose there exhibited, deserve all praise. There are of course some few incompetent and lazy officials, but the vast majority of our Indian administrators have the real good of the people at heart, and do their best to improve the condition of those committed to their charge. The pomp and glitter of the Viceregal Court must not blind us to the hard work daily done in all ranks of the Government, and we must gladly recognize the upright intentions and general success of the measures promulgated for the benefit of the peoples of India.

CHAPTER V.

I HAD to hasten away from the festivities of Lucknow, as my time seemed but short for all the sights I had still to see. So on the evening of December 1st I travelled on to Benares, which is distant about 200 miles from Lucknow. Benares is built on the banks of the Ganges, and is considered by the Hindus to be one of the holiest cities in India. In consequence the place is full of temples and shrines, and is a great resort of pilgrims. The population is over 175,000, which makes it the fifth most populous city in India. Like Athens of old, it may be said to be "wholly given to idolatry." The temples number more than 1000, and there are little shrines at the corners of all the streets. The streets are extremely narrow, often only four feet wide, and the houses high. The city is crowded with strangers from all parts of India, and is said to be a great resort of criminals. Certainly in these narrow and crowded quarters anyone might remain for a long time undiscovered, while the constant coming and going of numbers of pilgrims make it impossible for the police to know all the inhabitants. Within the the city the police number about one to every 300 of the population, which is about three-and-a-half times as many as the proportion in London.

The great feature of Benares is the river-front. Just at this point on the Ganges there is a cliff about 80 feet high, and on the slope of this the city is built. For about three miles along the bank there is a constant succession of stone palaces and temples, from each of which there are broad stone steps leading down to the brink of the water. These great staircases are called "ghâts," and are used by the pilgrims as bathing places. At all hours of the day, but especially in the early morning, these splendid flights of steps are crowded with countless throngs of bathers, wbo wash themselves in the water, and believe that they thus obtain cleansing from their sins. Men and women walk down the steps, and without unclothing themselves, immerse their bodies in the stream, and then reascend the ghât, having thus accomplished the object of their pilgrimage. These ghâts have been built by various Rajahs and Princes of India, and they often lead up to a palace, which is occupied by the owner, when he comes at intervals to bathe in the sacred river. As each palace is built on a different design, and as there are also many splendid temples on the bank, the river-front of Benares is wonderfully picturesque. When the broad flights of steps are thronged with bathers, dressed in bright coloured garments, the scene is one of the most striking to be seen in India.

During my visit these ghâts were illuminated in honour of Lady Ripon, who was staying at Benares. The illumination is done in the simplest way, but the effect is most beautiful. Thousands and thousands of little clay saucers are filled with oil, in which there floats a wick. These saucers are then placed in long lines along every stair of every ghât, and along the balconies, and roofs, and window-sills of the houses. Then when all are lighted the effect is most striking. We went in a boat on the river, so that we might get a good view of the whole illumination. For about two miles along the river-front every cornice, and window, and balcony, and every stair of every ghât was picked out with long lines of little twinkling lights. The night was dark and still, so that there was nothing to mar the full effect of the scene. The thousands of lights enabled one to notice the crowds of spectators, who watched the state barge, which carried Lady Ripon, pass down the long line of lit-up palaces. As this way of illumination necessarily follows the lines of the architecture of the building, it is much more pleasing and effective than the number of incongruous and trashy designs which disfigure the streets of London when we attempt any illuminations. Nothing could be prettier than the long steep staircases, every stair of which was studded with lights. The varied outlines of the buildings, and the cliff with its crowded roofs, and the innumerable lights were all reflected in the water, and thus the beauty of the scene was increased by the picturesque character of the site of the city itself.

The buildings of Benares are not specially fine. The temples appear mean and poor when compared with the beautiful buildings of Delhi and Agra, or with the great structures of Southern India. But they are noticeable from the crowds of worshippers who throng their courts. They are used, and Hinduism is here seen as a living religion. Every shrine and every image in Benares is worshipped and adored. Every temple is crowded with pilgrims, who are there as real worshippers for the purpose of praying to the gods. Amongst these the Golden Temple is one of the most famous. It is a small building, surrounded with houses, and of no great beauty. It gets its name from its domes, which were overlaid with gold by Runjeet Singh. But though its size and architectural pretensions are in no way remarkable, yet one could not help noticing the throngs of worshippers which were constantly passing in and out. The whole of the courts and rooms seemed always full of people. As one left, another took his place, and successive worshippers were praying and prostrating themselves all through the day before the idol shrines. There seemed to be a constant chant of priests, and on all sides one saw fakirs smeared with clay and with long tangled hair, nearly naked and very dirty, who recited prayers all day long. The central idol to which all this worship was addressed was the "lingam," or phallic emblem, said to typify the creative principle, but the cause and apology for every kind of immorality. The reproductive energy of nature was also symbolized by a great figure of a bull carved in stone about seven feet high. Round the central court under a colonnade many sacred bulls were tethered. These animals used to roam about the streets, and put their noses into every grain shop, and help themselves to anything they could find. They were hardly driven away by the shopkeepers, even when their depredations became excessive, as these temple bulls are considered specially sacred. But a later Government regulation has ordered that they should be kept from straying about the streets, so that the traffic may not be impeded.

These are not the only animals reverenced in Benares. There is a building, popularly called the Monkey Temple, which is crowded with thousands of these "living deities." They are considered to be sacred, and are fed by everyone who enters the building. The result of this is that they are as bold as possible, and as soon as anyone enters they rush from all parts, expecting the sweetmeats, which are sold on the spot by enterprising salesmen. These monkeys are of a dark orange colour, and are of all ages and sizes. One was pointed out, who was supposed to be the strongest, and to rule over the rest. He certainly seemed ready to exercise his power, and robbed the others whenever he got the chance. The whole pack of them quarrelled, and fought, and bit at each other, and the noise was anything but pleasing. They scrambled and climbed over the roofs and pinnacles of the building, and scampered over the floors, clinging on all sides to the carved pillars, and ever watching for the offerings made to them by the faithful. The temple itself is dedicated to the goddess Durga, who is venerated as the wife of Siva. Here again the worship paid to her was no perfunctory performance. While we were there, a poor woman, looking very ill, entered and prostrated herself before the figure of the goddess. My native guide, who was a Police Inspector, and could talk English, happened to know this woman.

She belonged to Calcutta, but had come on this wearisome pilgrimage, and was now engaged in going round all the famous shrines and temples in Benares, having to pay fees at each to the priests, and before every idol she made her prayer for health. When she had visited all the temples, she would return to Calcutta, having spent all that she had, and one fears she would be "nothing bettered but rather grown worse."

This native Police Inspector was an intelligent person; he had been told off to look after me by my kind host, and he was a most efficient guide. He spoke of coming to England some day, and was most anxious to hear about our manners and customs. His clothes were of English cloth made partly in native fashion, but he wore trousers and English shoes. He was a Hindu by religion, and when we entered the temples belonging to his own faith, he slipped off his shoes. But when we came to the great Mohammedan mosque, which is one of the great sights of Benares, he acted very differently. There, as a Police Inspector, he demanded to enter with his shoes on. He spoke roughly to the caretaker, and almost insisted on his right to do as he liked. His European clothes seemed to make him partly an Englishman, and he wished to be treated as such. For there was no desire on the part of the caretaker of the mosque to force me to take off my boots. I was to be allowed to enter with covered feet. The "sahibs" always did so. But the Hindustani people were always made to come in barefooted, or not at all. The argument lasted for some time, but at last my guide said that I must go into the mosque by myself, as he would not take off his boots, and they would not allow him to enter without doing so.

The different way in which this Hindu acted at the two sacred places was no doubt determined by something more than religious feeling. The great mosque at Benares is a standing reminder to them of the fact that they were conquered by the Mohammedans. It was built by the Emperor Aurangzeb on the site of a Hindu temple, and is thus an offence to all who belong to that religion. The mosque itself is noticeable for its slender minarets, which are 147 feet high. I ascended one of these for the sake of the view. The ascent itself was a little difficult. The tower was so slender that the steps of the winding staircase were only two feet long, measuring from the wall to the central pillar. Of course the part nearest the wall was the only place wide enough to step upon, and thus one clambered up with difficulty, and it would have been impossible to pass any other person on the staircase. One's elbows touched the stones on each side, and it was almost like ascending the shaft of a tall chimney. But the view from the top was well worth the labour. The whole city lay below, the river could be seen for a long distance, the ghâts crowded with bathers, the temples and palaces, the distant country, and the opposite bank, were all spread before one like a map, while round one's head green parrots flew and screamed, who seemed to have their nests in the holes of the masonry. The mosque with its slender minarets is built high above the bank of the river, and is approached by a steep staircase, which makes it a striking object in all views of Benares.

One of the most curious buildings in the city is the Observatory of Jai Sing. On its flat roof there are several stone astronomical instruments of gigantic size for taking observations. There are the remains of dials, and quadrants, and mural circles, built of stone, most accurately set up, which were used by native astronomers for determining the position of the stars and planets.

Besides its temples and ghâts, Benares is also famous for its manufactures. Its brass work is well known in England, and lacquered toys for children are also exported to the West. But the most expensive handicraft, which is wrought in the city, is the "kincob" work. This is gold or silver thread woven into silk or cotton fabrics, making a sort of brocade, which is most rich. The natives admire this work extremely. The thinner "kincob" is used fot women's veils and dresses, while the thicker stuffs make trousers and dress pieces for men. The gold and silver thread is made of pure metal, and when the stuff into which it has been woven is worn out, the garment is burnt and the metal carefully saved for future use. The preciousness of the material makes the stuff very expensive, and I was shown some pieces which were worth £3 a yard! English ladies have not yet learned to use it, though I heard of one Court dress, where the upper skirt was made of this brocade, and was much admired.

Benares is the centre of popular modern Hinduism. There may be much that is beautiful in the old Vedic hymns and Sanskrit literature of very early times, but there is little that is worth preserving in modern Hinduism, and the degradation and impurity of much of the popular religion is nowhere more noticeable than it is in this city. I may quote here a few sentences from the late Rev. M. A. Sherring, who laboured for thirty years in Benares. He writes thus about idolatry: "The nature of the Hindu partakes of the supposed nature of the gods whom he worships. And what is that nature? According to the traditions handed about amongst the natives, and constantly dwelt upon in their conversation, and referred to in their popular songs—which perhaps would be sufficient proof—yet more especially according to the numberless statements and narratives found in their sacred writings, on which these traditions are based, it is, in many instances, vile and abominable in the last degree. Idolatry is a word denoting all that is wicked in imagination and impure in practice." Certainly the sacred objects of worship exposed in the temples of Benares cannot tend to spiritualize or ennoble the worshippers. They must deaden and deprave all those who come into contact with such a religion.

From Benares I had a long railway journey of 475 miles to Calcutta. The time taken was about eighteen hours, and the line lay through a very thickly populated country. Every acre seemed cultivated, and the land was occupied in every corner. The population is, I believe, thicker in Lower Bengal than in any other part of India, and in some districts there are 900 people to the square mile. I had very little opportunity of seeing Calcutta, as I only stopped long enough for a bath and breakfast, and then drove across the city to take the train for Darjeeling. I had been advised to hasten there as quickly as possible, as the weather in the hills becomes unsettled about the middle of December, and the nights very cold. The great sight of Darjeeling is the view of the snowclad peaks, but later on in the winter these are often obscured by rain and mists for days together. It would have been disappointing to arrive at that hill station and find oneself in the clouds. So I was advised to hurry onwards for fear of losing the fine weather.

The distance from Calcutta to Darjeeling is about 350 miles. The first part of the journey lies through a flat and uninteresting country. At sunset we reached the Ganges, which we crossed by a steam ferry, and entered another train, which was waiting. We travelled all through the night, and in the early morning found ourselves at the foot of the hills. Then began the great interest of the journey, viz., the climb up the lower slopes of the Himalayas to the plateau on which Darjeeling is built. This is effected by a very narrow gauge railway with extremely powerful engines. The gauge is only two-and-a-half feet, and the carriages are five-and-a-half feet broad, and thus project on each side beyond the wheels. By means of this narrow gauge the train is enabled to go round very sharp curves, and thus to ascend the hill in steep zigzags. The distance from Siliguri at the foot of the hills to Darjeeling is 48 miles, and this distance is accomplished in eight hours, during which one ascends about 7000 feet. It was the most beautiful railway journey I ever took. At first we passed through a broad strip of swampy jungle, called the Terai, at the foot of the hills, which is so malarious and unhealthy that none can live in it, and in many parts it is the home of the tiger and rhinoceros. Then as the ascent began, the hills on each side were seen covered with dense wood and undergrowth. Creepers twined everywhere, often with stems as thick as small trees. Butterflies of gorgeous colours flew about through the undergrowth, and far above one got glimpses of heights still to be ascended. Often we could see the track above our heads round which we were presently to wind, and long distances had to be traversed in the zigzag to win a very small rise in perpendicular height. Often the rail ran alongside the mountain road or pass, which had been used from time immemorial, and then one saw numbers of the hill men, journeying to or from Tibet with strings of small active ponies, laden with merchandise. This was the only method a few years ago, before the railway was made, for supplying Darjeeling with stores, and these are still the only merchants who cross the high passes of the Himalayas, and penetrate into the unknown country beyond our northern frontier. Wild looking, dark-faced, wiry men they appeared, and each was armed with a long knife or short sword in a wooden sheath, which could be used either for cutting food or hacking down branches in the jungle, or as a weapon of offence very dangerous at close quarters.

As we got higher the view over the plains beneath was spread before us like a map. We could look far to the southward, and see the rich flat land with winding streams and cultivated fields shut out from the cold north by

> "The stainless ramps of huge Himâla's wall."

We passed many tea plantations, but at this season of the year there was little to be done except weeding.

The planters' houses were built on various spurs or level plateaux on the slopes, and although two tea gardens might be in sight of one another, yet the intervening valleys were often so deep that a ride from one to the other was a matter of several miles. The tea plants looked like low bushes about one to two feet high, planted in rows like strawberry plants, with broad passages between the rows. As we got higher still we came into the regions of the rhododendron and tree ferns. These last were great spreading plants, and seemed to flourish luxuriantly in the heat and moisture of these hill regions. The reason why the vegetation is everywhere so rich is because the rainfall is so excessive. There are places in Assam where from 30 to 40 *feet* of rain fall every year, and in one year 805 inches were measured. This enormous rainfall aided by the intense heat causes all parts of the lower ranges of the hills to be clothed in forest. The very trunks of the trees support other plants, and the branches are everywhere beautified with moss and ferns, sweet tresses of orchid blossoms, and long creepers. Unluckily our last piece of the ascent was made through clouds. The edge of the ridge on which Darjeeling stands was enveloped in a thick damp mist, and we feared that we should get no view of the distant hills. But it was only a local belt of cloud which hung over the extreme edge of the ridge, and as we ran into Darjeeling Station the sun was shining brightly, and we had a full view of the perpetual snows.

Darjeeling is a small town built on a ridge, bounded on three sides by valleys which are in places 6000 feet deep. The houses are perched at various elevations on the adjacent slopes. The majority of them are detached bungalows, and the owners have built them so as to command the best views. There is a short piece of flat road, but wheeled conveyances are rare, and the majority of Europeans ride, or are carried about in palanquins. One's luggage was carried from the station by female porters, who seemed capable of supporting enormous weights. They carried everything on their backs, supporting their load by means of a band, which passed across the forehead. These hardworking wives of the hill-men seem to do all the work of porterage, and were the chief carriers who brought supplies to the various bungalows. The natives of this part of India are called Bhutiás, and are of a Tibeto-Burman stock. They are probably one of the aboriginal races of India, which were overcome by the Aryan immigrations. They have a very Chinese caste of features with high cheek bones, and eyes at an angle to the nose, and are dressed in Chinese clothes. They are Buddhists in religion, and seem to have been driven from the lowlands to these hill regions by the stronger Aryan tribes, who invaded India in very early times.

The territory of Darjeeling was ceded to us by the Rajah of Sikkim and is surrounded by independent territory. Nepâl is on the west and Sikkim on the east, while to the north lie the unexplored regions of Tibet. One heard much of the difficulty of penetrating into the country north of our frontier. The inhabitants of Tibet are most jealous of strangers, no European is allowed to cross the boundary, and the passes through the Himalayas are almost unknown. The wonderful city and monastery of Lhassa which lies only some 200 miles from Darjeeling has (I believe) not been visited by any European in this century. The Jesuit Abbé Huc got there, but nowadays the danger is greater, and Englishmen are forbidden to attempt the expedition. At Lhassa the great Lama lives, who is the head of Chinese Buddhism, and who is said to wear always a gold mask so that no eye may see his features. He is supposed to be an incarnation of Buddha, and when he dies, the monks discover some infant, into whom they say the spirit of Buddha has passed, and he becomes the great Lama. This Lamaism is a very low type of Buddhism, and is in many points contrary to the teaching of

Gautama. It is a great erection of priestly power, for since 1419 the Dalai Lama has been sole temporal sovereign of Tibet.* But its gorgeous ritual and gross superstitions, its prayer-wheels and powerful hierarchy are all degradations of original Buddhism. The monks and priests have overlaid the spiritual doctrines of Gautama with later inventions, and the purity and beauty of the original teaching has been lost.

This is, however, not the place to sketch the rise and progress of Buddhism. Only when one was so near the frontier, and comparatively such a short distance from the great cathedral and monastery of Lhassa, one could not help enquiring about the people beyond our northern border. Although Englishmen are forbidden to enter Tibet, yet something is done in the way of exploration. There is a school at Darjeeling where natives are trained in surveying and map drawing, and these in the disguise of merchants or traders are able to penetrate into Tibet. They are exposed to great dangers, for if their object was discovered they would be murdered, as the inhabitants of Tibet are most fearful of strangers. But these explorers are able to pass our frontier without suspicion, and often bring back most valuable results. One had recently returned after three years' wanderings with most important sketches of the unknown parts of Tibet. Another had been dwelling for some time in Lhassa, and had seen the mysterious abode of the great Lama. But these discoveries are not openly published. The routes are mapped, and the observations stored away in the Indian Intelligence Department, and thus they will be useful for military or political purposes, if they are ever needed. But the explorers' names are kept secret, as their lives would hardly be safe, and certainly their usefulness would be gone, if they were known to be obtaining such intelligence.

* See Rhys David's *Buddhism, passim.*

The chief beauty of Darjeeling lies in the views of the snowy range obtainable from it, and political considerations were forgotten in feasting one's eyes on the magnificent prospect spread out before one. The ridge on which the town is built runs northwards towards the snows, but after it has extended for about half-a-mile it terminates abruptly in a steep slope. Thus the end of the ridge forms a sort of bastion from the edge of which one gains an uninterrupted view of Kinchingunga, the second highest mountain in the world. Immediately beneath one's feet there is a steep slope, leading down into a valley, some 6000 feet deep. On each side there are similar valleys, the slopes of which are in places covered with tea gardens, but which gradually sink down into far-off depths and rocky ravines, into which the whole of the English and Scotch mountains might be thrown without filling up their vast recesses. On the left hand these valleys are bounded by a range of hills, 12,000 feet high, which are from six to twenty miles distant, and which block any further view in that direction. On the right the hills are farther away, and the main range of snowclad heights can be traced for many miles. In front is the great mass of Kinchingunga itself. It is fifty miles off, yet the clearness of the air enables us to trace every ravine, and precipice, and splintered crag. The skyline of the peaks is specially picturesque, and is boldly defined against the blue heavens. The total height is over 28,000 feet, the valleys beneath one's feet were some 6000 feet deep, and the plateau on which one stood was some 7000 feet above sea level. Thus looking first downwards and then upwards, one could see about 27,000 of perpendicular height. The line of perpetual snow begins at about 18,000 feet. The grandest view I obtained was from the back part of the ridge, from a point called Jalapaher Hill. This hill is some two miles from the station, and about 900 feet higher than the town of Darjeeling. From this point the whole country was spread before one like a map, and seldom have I seen a greater portion of the earth's surface at one view. Miles of ridges and valleys seemed to stretch on all sides. At one's feet was the town of Darjeeling, and beyond that there were successive ranges of hills more and more distant, till at last high above all towered the great mass of Kinchingunga, seeming to fill up half the sky with its snows. On the left over another ridge there peeped a little triangle of snow, and this was the peak of Everest, eighty miles away, the highest mountain in the world, which could just be seen over the intervening ridge. I heard that the view of Everest from this ridge was grand in the extreme, and many travellers make an expedition to the top of these hills (which are 12,000 feet high) to gain a full view of the giant mountain. I had to be content with the peep I obtained of him from afar, but the second highest mountain satisfied my aspirations of the beautiful.

Another lovely walk round Birch Hill completed my Darjeeling experiences. The hill itself is clothed with thick vegetation, and the ferns and creepers nourished by the constant trickling streams, which flow down its steep sides, cover the rock with green tracery. The sunset-glow on Kinchingunga lingered long after the valleys were in deep shadow, and as the mists curled up from the lower grounds, and the light faded on the eternal snows, I saw a sight which I can never forget. The summer residence of the Lieutenant-Governor of Bengal is built on Birch Hill, and one of the chief delights of this coveted office must be the possession of a house from which such views can be obtained. This Lieutenant-Governorship is the highest prize of the Civil Service in India, and not the least pleasant part of its tenure is the consideration that every summer can be spent in the pure air and lovely surroundings of the Governor's house at Darjeeling.

As the light faded I returned to the town. Below in the native quarter I heard a gong beaten in front

N

of a Buddhist temple. Each evening this noise was kept up for about an hour, as part of a religious worship. This northern or Chinese Buddhism is a low and degraded religion, very different from the more philosophical faith which the followers of Buddha believe elsewhere. Of course even amongst the Tibetan Lamas there are said to be learned and devout monks, who have pried into the secrets of nature, and have discovered esoteric doctrines, which are not revealed to the vulgar. These are now being examined by certain Englishmen in India, and the Theosophists of Simla are said to have become possessors of certain mystical and abstruse doctrines, unknown to the uninitiated. But leaving these wonderful doctrines on one side, and speaking only of the Buddhistic faith as held by the common people, one could not find much to praise in the religion professed by the hill tribes at Darjeeling. It was a gain to have left behind the Hindu idols of Lower India, but the superstitions resorted to by the Lepchas and Bhotias were very unspiritual. Praying wheels were in common use amongst them. These are metal drums which revolve on an axis, and which are filled with prayers written on parchment. The worshipper, who causes such a praying wheel to rotate, is considered to have repeated all the prayers which are contained in the drum. As many times as he turns the wheel round, so many times is he supposed to have offered up all the prayers contained in it. Thus he easily gains the credit of being a prayerful person. Others write their prayers on flags or strips of cotton. These are fastened on poles, and left to flutter in the wind, the idea being that as the breeze shakes the flags, so the good of the prayers is set free, and this redounds to the credit of the setter-up of the flags. These and other like superstitions have nothing to do with the pure doctrines of original Buddhism, but are excrescences and abuses which have been invented by the Lamas of Tibet. While such superstitious practices are encouraged and fostered amongst the common people by the priests, the religion can do but little for the spiritual life of its followers.

From Darjeeling I returned to Calcutta, again seeing the wonderful views of the mountain sides, as the line wound down the slopes. It was after sunset as we passed through the Terai belt at the foot of the hills, and the swarms of fireflies in the long grass of the swamps were most remarkable. Then another long night journey over the plains of Eastern Bengal brought me to Calcutta about noonday.

Calcutta, though the capital of India and the central seat of the Government, has not much to reward the ardent sightseer. The city is comparatively modern, having been founded in 1686 by the East India Company, who built a factory at this point on the river Húghli, and afterwards defended it by a fort. These factories were houses of trade, where the goods obtained from inland were exchanged for the European commodities which the traders brought from across the seas. Round this factory at Calcutta there was gradually formed a town, which has steadily increased in size, and now extends for some considerable distance along both banks of the Húghli, and with its suburbs numbers over 776,000 in population. The chief reason for this great prosperity is the commanding position which the city occupies. It stands on the bank of a river which is navigable for the largest ships. The Húghli is one of the mouths of the Ganges, and Calcutta is built about eighty miles from the sea. Thus it always could be securely approached, and vessels could discharge or take in their cargoes from lighters laden with goods from the interior, which had been cheaply and safely brought down by the stream of the Ganges. Standing on the edge of the river one sees numbers of large steamers anchored in the stream. The river is tidal and about as wide as the Thames at London Bridge. The steamers for two miles down the river were anchored three and four deep, and the number of large vessels in the river must have been nearly a hundred.

The city of Calcutta consists of the native quarter, the public buildings, and the houses occupied by the European residents. The streets in the native quarter are generally wide and well paved, though in some of the poorer parts the population is very thickly crowded together and the smells in the hot weather are not very agreeable. The public buildings are fine. The new Law Courts, the Telegraph and Post Offices, and the Town Hall, are handsome structures. Government House, which is the winter residence of the Viceroy, stands in the midst of the European quarter. It is a large and commodious building, said by Fergusson to be copied in design from Keddlestone Hall in Derbyshire, a house built in the latter half of the last century, whose architects were the brothers Adam. Its style is Classical, with large pillars forming a colonnade which extends round the building. In the centre are the state-rooms under a lofty dome. Connected with this central structure there are four detached wings appropriated to the private apartments, and joined by semicircular galleries to the state-rooms. Thus the Palace is very convenient, as the portion in which the Viceroy and his family, and secretaries reside is entirely distinct from the reception-rooms and state apartments. At an evening party given by the Viceroy, after a Drawing-Room, I saw these large rooms lighted up and filled with a gay crowd, in which uniforms largely predominated, and the effect was very striking.

The Cathedral is a less successful building. It was designed under Bishop Wilson, and before the principles of Gothic architecture were properly understood. The result is a poor design, mean in its details, and pretentious without dignity. From a distance the spire has a good effect, but there are neither aisles nor transepts, which causes the interior to look like a large square hall. But though the building itself is thus unlovely, the service was reverently performed, the congregation was large, and the choir sang well. Round the walls there were numerous tablets to the memory of those who had succumbed to the unhealthiness of the climate of Calcutta, and of many military men who had died in various parts of India. Amongst these memorial tablets, I noticed the one to Lady Canning, the wife of a former Viceroy, and those to Bishops Wilson, Cotton, and Milman. In one way Calcutta has always been pre-eminent in its Bishops. All have died at their posts. Not one has returned to England to live at ease. After having once put their hands to the plough there has been no looking back. This is a fact which can be said of no other of our foreign dioceses, and the spiritual effect of such unflinching self-denial and perseverance to the end must be felt beneficially by the whole Church in India.

Missionary work in Calcutta is not neglected, and amongst other efforts the work of the Oxford Mission is noticeable. This is a Brotherhood sent out by the University of Oxford to do for Calcutta what the Cambridge Mission is doing for Delhi. Its main idea is to influence and try to convert to Christianity the English-speaking Babu, many of whom are employed in the various Government offices. "Babu" is a title given to the educated natives, numbers of whom reside in the city; many have passed through the Calcutta University course, and all understand some English. This large and increasing class have in many instances given up their old idolatrous practices, and are seeking for a purer faith. Amongst them has been started the Brahmo Somaj, which is an eclectic religion, in which Christ has a place as a human teacher, and whose members insist on the Unity and the Fatherhood of God. In England it is best known through the preaching of Babu Cheshub Chunder Sen, but in Calcutta several of his co-religionists have parted company from him in consequence of his devising new developments of doctrine, which they think minister rather to his vanity than to edification. This Somaj is embraced by many of the more thoughtful of the Hindus, and the Oxford Mission may do much for them. Besides these there are a large number of English-speaking natives, who have given up religion altogether. They have learnt the folly of idolatry, but Western literature has also opened to them scores of infidel and agnostic books in which the Christian religion is vilified and ridiculed. These have been greedily devoured by those who desired to break free from all restraints. Students of the Calcutta University read Tom Paine and the deistical literature of the last century. They read translations of the latest German and French controversial literature, and the writings of modern sceptics, and the result has been that many of the English-speaking natives of India have no religion at all. They are merely simple Materialists, with one desire to get up in the world and amass wealth. Here again is a large class for whom the Oxford Mission can do much. Their arguments, which are often shallow, can be met and answered by lectures, and discussions, and books, and they may thus be brought back to the knowledge of God. It is not altogether a hopeless task, for no man can be satisfied to rest long in blank atheism. He must desire to know something about God and the hereafter. The human instincts are on the side of faith, and thus the Oxford Missionaries find souls desirous of being taught. Their work is too new yet to show great results, but the Community seemed hopeful. Of course many inquirers come merely to discuss, and argue, and exhibit their learning, and air their English. But there are some who seem more in earnest. In Calcutta there are all sorts and conditions of natives, and the Christian missionary owes a debt to the educated as well as to the uneducated, to the "Greek" as well as to the "barbarian." Certainly if anyone can be called the "Greek" of India, it is the inquiring, quick, subtle, shallow Babu, whose mind is stuffed with undigested knowledge, and who is always desirous to tell or to hear some new thing. To him also the Gospel has a message; all honour to those who are trying to interpret it and bring it home to him.

The fashionable part of Calcutta, where the best houses are situated, is called Chowringhee. This is a broad street with houses on one side, and on the other a wide "Maidan," or plain, kept as a recreation ground or park. Here riders find ample galloping ground, volunteers drill, troops exercise, games are played, and walkers lounge. The street is always full of life. On every side is seen the ubiquitous "bhîsti," who with his sheepskin full of water on his back lets the stream squirt forth over the road, and thus lays the dust. Carriages pass by drawn by handsome "walers" (which is the name given to horses bred in Australia). Natives in various costumes stare up at the great houses in which the "sahibs" live. While far across the green plain a line of light is reflected from the river, and tall masts mark the place where rows of ships lie anchored in the broad stream. Beyond them are seen the houses in Howrah, which is a crowded suburb on the opposite bank of the Húghli. The prettiest part of this wide plain has been laid out as a public garden. Here in the evening after sunset the English walk to hear the band play, and to breathe the fresh air which blows off the river. The electric light makes the place as light as day, and the big ships lie close to the bank, adding to the picturesqueness of the scene.

The finest gardens in Calcutta are the Botanical Gardens, which are kept up by Government. Here are wonderful orchid houses, groups of sago palms, a banyan tree (said to be the largest in the world), which with its re-rooted branches covers an acre of ground, and avenues and flowering shrubs of the prettiest kinds. It is like Kew Gardens under a tropical sky and with no danger of frost. The most beautiful plants grow out of doors, and the flowers which have to be carefully cultivated in hothouses at home here grow in profusion.

On the left bank of the Húghli, in a suburb called Garden Reach, is the palace where the ex-King of Oudh still lives in the enjoyment of a pension of £120,000 a year. He was deposed in 1856 by Lord Dalhousie, and his dominions annexed. For nearly thirty years the old ruffian has dwelt in luxury. He has collected his family and retainers round him, and spends his time in gathering together a menagerie of wild beasts. This part of Calcutta has been deserted by the richer Europeans, as the quietness and respectability of the quarter has not been improved by the patronage bestowed upon it by this dissolute ex-monarch.

Calcutta compares favourably with many European capitals. Its streets are wide, its trade enormous, its shops well filled, its public buildings fine, and its statues (*mirabile dictu*) really works of art. The inhabitants comprise representatives of all races. English sailors and Chinese dealers, American tourists and Australian traders, are seen in its streets. Here too is to be found the pleasantest and most cultured English society in India. Here is the centre of gaiety as well as the seat of Government. The English have never received sufficient honour as great founders of cities. But here we can see how within two hundred years has grown up a town which exceeds in population any other in India, and probably far outnumbers anything ever conceived by the Great Mogul. Starting from the small factory and fort erected by the East India Company for the purposes of trade, there is now a large and well built city of nearly 800,000 inhabitants. Calcutta, which Macaulay called "the city of palaces," is a proof of the growth and expansion of England, which is undeniable.

CHAPTER VI.

AS I had to be in Rangoon by Christmas-Day, I was obliged to cut short my visit to Calcutta, and on the evening of December 13th I went on board the British Indian Company's s.s. *Pemba*, which was lying in the river ready to start for Burma the following morning, as soon as the English mail arrived. The mosquitoes in the cabins were very bloodthirsty, but by carefully tucking in the curtains round my berth, I had a good night. Calcutta from its nearness to the Húghli is always full of these pests, and on the river itself they are specially numerous and seemed hungry. In the morning we dropped down the river with the tide, and soon were slipping past the palaces at Garden Reach, the ships at anchor, and the last streets and houses of the suburbs of Calcutta. We had a quick run down the 80 miles of the Húghli between flat and ever-widening banks, and before sunset we were on the open sea of the Bay of Bengal. The distance from Calcutta to Rangoon is 1000 miles, and the voyage takes about three days.

The following is a short account of the history of Burma and of the way in which it was annexed by the English. Burma lies to the east of the Bay of Bengal, and is bounded by China on the north and by Siam on the east. This great tract of country is peopled by a race of Tibeto-Chinese origin, and has a history of its own reaching back to very early times. There were constant wars in this region, various invaders overran the country both from north and south, and it was divided into several kingdoms. These were consolidated into one in the year 1750 by a king called Alompra, who founded his capital at Ava, on the Irrawaddy, and whose decendants still reign in Upper

Burma. His successors, not satisfied with their own territory, made raids into British India, and finally war was declared in 1824. This first Burmese war made us masters of the Provinces of Arakan and Tennasserim, which are the districts extending along the sea-coast from India to the Malay Peninsula, excepting the land about Rangoon, at the mouth of the Irrawaddy, which still remained in the possession of the King of Burma. This arrangement lasted till the year 1852, when the second Burmese war broke out in consequence of the ill-treatment of English merchants at Rangoon, and the refusal by the King of any redress. The war was short and decisive, the Burmese soldiers were no match for the disciplined English and native troops sent against them, and 200 miles of the valley of the Irrawaddy, from Rangoon to Prome, were occupied by the British forces. It was in storming a stockade at Rangoon that Lord Wolseley, then a young lieutenant, first distinguished himself under fire. After this war the province of Pegu, being the district containing the delta of the Irrawaddy, was annexed to the British dominions. Thus British Burma now consists of a strip of land extending along the sea-coast continuously from India to the Malay Peninsula. It contains over 80,000 square miles of territory, and commands all the ports and river-mouths of this region. Its inland border marches with independent Burma and Siam, and our frontier where it crosses the Irrawaddy, is some 200 miles from the sea. Thus the old kingdom of Ava has been driven entirely away from the sea-coast, and all the sea-borne trade is in the hands of the English. The present ruler of Upper Burma, King Theebaw, lives at Mandalay, a town near Ava, which he has made his new capital.

There are some curious statistics collected by Dr. W. W. Hunter to show how Burma has prospered since its annexation. Since 1852 Rangoon has become ten times as populous, and its trade has quadrupled in value. Other parts of the annexed territory have similarly increased, quiet and order have been established, and the people seem happy and contented. Akyab, which was a poor fishing village when we occupied the province in 1826, has now an annual trade valued at two millions sterling. Thus the comfort of the people has greatly increased since they have been under our rule.

On the morning of the third day after leaving Calcutta our steamer entered the Rangoon river, one of the mouths of the Irrawaddy, on which the town of Rangoon is built, some 20 miles from the sea. The Irrawaddy, which is about 1000 miles long, rises in the easternmost slopes of the Himalayas, in the unexplored country lying between Assam and China. It flows due south through the whole length of Burma, and falls into the sea through many mouths, which form the great delta of the river. As we steamed up the broad stream, we saw how flat the land was on either side, for all the country round has been made from silt brought down by the river and deposited in the sea. The jungle and growth on either side seemed thick, and much of the land was uncleared, though patches of rice were seen in places. As we drew nearer to Rangoon the great spire of the Golden Pagoda was seen from afar, dominating the town which lies at its foot. Coming still nearer we saw the wharves, houses, and landing stages, with the tower and spire of the Pro-Cathedral, a medium-sized Gothic church of no great architectural merit, built close to the water's edge. The river is nearly a mile wide at this point, and there were many ships lying at anchor in the stream. We were able to go alongside a wharf, and quickly found ourselves on shore.

Burma is a very interesting country to visit after India. The dissimilarity of the two places and of their inhabitants makes the comparison between them the more instructive. The first thing one notices is the people themselves. Instead of the dark-faced people of India, white-robed, quiet, and submissive, we have in Burma a light-coloured, lively race with a Chinese caste of features, and a bold, open, assured manner. They are very fond of bright colours, and the silk handkerchiefs which they tie round their heads are of the most brilliant tints of red and yellow, pink and green. The men wear a silk petticoat of bright colour, fastened round the waist and reaching to the calf of the leg, and above that a loose jacket. The women also wear silk clothes, and are addicted to bright colours. Their feet are bare, but shod with a loose sandal. Their heads are uncovered, and their long hair is tastefully arranged in large masses, and decorated with orchid tresses or other sweet-smelling flowers. There is none of the subjection or almost slavery of the woman common in India, where no respectable lady is ever seen in the streets unveiled. In Burma the women occupy a much freer and more independent position, they keep shops, go out marketing, and are as ready to chaffer and bargain as their Western sisters are at home. This fact of the enfranchisement of the women makes a Burmese crowd a much gayer sight than one in India, and when the bright-coloured clothes of both sexes, and the habit of wearing flowers are also remembered, the street scenes in Rangoon are always interesting.

Besides the Burmese inhabitants of the country there is also a strong contingent of Chinese. These industrious and keen-witted people are driving a thriving trade in Rangoon, their shops are well stored, and some of the streets in the town are entirely occupied by them. The sights in these streets were like what one has read about scenes in Canton. The way that elderly and respectable shop-keepers stood at their doors with nothing on but wide trowsers, a pair of spectacles, and a pigtail, and looked out on the world with a smile that was childlike and bland, transported one in thought into the Celestial Empire. Here too one saw their love of children and family life, and the publicity of their domestic arrangements. Whole households sat round tables, and drank their tea on the pavement in front of their houses, and the naked little ones ran about screaming with delight, very fat, with their little pigtails standing almost upright, and vibrating with excitement.

Besides the Chinese colony there is also a very large number of coolies from Southern India, who are tempted to cross the sea by the high rate of wages offered in Rangoon. The Burman considers himself much too great a personage to labour steadily for wages. He is uncertain in his temper, and liable to strike work at a moment's notice. He has not the plodding, quiet, obedient qualities which are required in a day labourer. Thus all the heavy work of loading ships, and carrying cargoes, and working in the rice mills, is done by coolies imported from Southern India. These dark-faced, sad-looking Tamils, work for a few years and then return to their own villages with the money they have earned in Burma. Thus Burmese, Chinese and Tamils jostle each other in the streets of Rangoon, and each race follows its own customs without interfering with those of the others. Sometimes also the crowd is increased by the presence of Karens or Shâns from the interior. These are a darker and more savage race, who were probably the original inhabitants of the country, before it was overrun by the Burmese. They wear cloth garments, and seldom stay long in the towns. They inhabit the thick forests and jungles of the interior, clearing scanty patches by burning down the trees, and then sowing their rice amongst the ashes. They are prone to Nât or Devil-worship, but numbers are now Christianized through the labours of both American and English missionaries.

The English quarter of Rangoon is away from the river on somewhat higher ground. Here the houses of the Europeans stand, each in its own compound. The houses are built entirely of teak wood, as stone is almost unknown. Many are raised on piles, as the rainfall is so excessive, that the lower story is seldom dry enough to be inhabited. The compounds looked very green after the burnt-up plains of India, and were full of tall trees and flowering shrubs. The croton and the coleus filled the garden beds with colour, beautiful creepers gay with flowers covered the porches, and in many houses were seen the flowering orchids attached to pieces of wood and suspended in the air, for which Burma is famous. These flourish well in the heat and damp, and many new sorts have been discovered in the jungles of the interior.

The English residents in Rangoon consist chiefly of the Government officials, the military officers, and the merchants who have settled there for purposes of trade. The head of the Government is called the Chief Commissioner, who is a civilian appointed from the Bengal Presidency. The chief export of Burma is rice, which is grown in great quantities all through the delta. The part under cultivation has greatly increased since we have had the country, but it is still only a small portion of the entire area. Out of 80,000 square miles of our territory only about 9000 are cultivated. This is partly caused by the scantiness of the population, which is a little over three millions. There are also very few roads, most of the land being uncleared. The numerous creeks and river mouths make land travelling in the delta almost impossible, and the ordinary mode of conveyance is by boat. There is one short railway of 164 miles from Rangoon to Prome, but this is the only line which is made at present. The rainfall is enormous, and from May to October the whole delta is under water, and travelling in the interior is almost impossible. The jungle, composed of bamboo and thick undergrowth, is difficult of penetration at all times, but during the rains it is impassable.

The country being so wet, the most profitable crop is rice. The Burman clears a patch of ground on the edge of one of the numerous streams which intersect the delta, and sows his seed just before the rainy season commences. When the country is flooded with rain, the rice-plant begins to shoot and grow. It flourishes only where the soil is saturated with rain, and where the water remains on the surface of the ground. The long green stalks shoot up through the water, and grow to a height of between two and three feet, and the grain is ripe when the rainy season is over. When the crop is cut, if it is to be exported to England, it is packed in boats and carried by water to the mill. There are many of these rice mills built along the banks of the river and creek on which Rangoon stands. In the mill the grain (or "paddy" as it is called) goes through three processes. It is first sifted to cleanse it from dirt, then it has its outer husk removed, and lastly the inner envelope round the rice is stripped off. This last process, which leaves the grain quite white and ready for use, is not done to the rice which has to make a long sea voyage, for the white rice would ferment and lose its colour. So generally the inner envelope is left on the grain, and it undergoes this final process in the mills in England.

Besides the rice trade there is also a large exportation of timber. There are large forests of teak and other valuable trees, which grow in the interior of the country and are under the control of the Government Forest Department. The revenue from this source amounts to over £160,000 a year, and thus the forest lands of Burma are a great source of wealth. The logs, when cut, are floated down the rivers in large rafts, which are stranded opposite to the saw mills. There they are received by trained elephants, who drag the logs from the river, and take them to the saws, and pile them up in large stacks to await shipment to England.

Besides the great difference both in dress and appearance visible between the Burmese and the people of India, they also differ in their religion. The Burmese are pure Buddhists, and it may be well to give a short outline of this widespread religion. The founder of it was a man of royal race called Siddhattha, surnamed Gautama, who was born about the middle of the sixth century B.C., somewhere in the north of Oudh. His early life was spent in quiet luxury, and he had everything that heart could desire. When he was 29 years old he left all, wife and home, riches and luxury, and went forth as a mendicant, with shaved head and yellow robe, to live a wandering and ascetic life. For seven years he wandered, seeking to find peace for his soul, and listening to the spiritual directions of various teachers. All was of no avail, self-mortification did not bring him deliverance, the goal was not yet reached. But at last, sitting under a tree, which in after ages became a sacred spot, he found illumination, and learnt the secret of happiness, and how deliverance from suffering was to be attained. This moment in the life of Gautama is the turning point of his life. From henceforth he was called "Buddha" or the Enlightened One, and his life was spent in preaching to others the secret which he had discovered. He soon began to convert others to his way of thinking, he gathered round him faithful disciples, and he thus started a religion, which was essentially of a missionary type. He died about the age of eighty, leaving his doctrines to be further propagated by his followers. Gradually the religion grew and spread, until all India was converted to the Buddhistic faith. From India to Ceylon, from Ceylon to Burma, and on to Siam, and Java, and Sumatra, the tidings spread. Northwards and eastwards, to Tibet and China, Buddhist preachers carried their doctrines, till all these countries were converted to this faith. But while it was thus winning its way in other countries, in its native land of India Buddhism lost its power. Brahmanism, with its idol shrines and caste peculiarities, fought long with it for the dominion of India, and "for the last thousand years Buddhism has been a banished religion from its native home." * But though exiled from India it has triumphed in other lands, and it has been calculated that five hundred millions of people, nearly half of the inhabitants of the world, still follow the teaching of Gautama Buddha.

What then is this religion which has so wonderfully influenced the world's beliefs? What were the doctrines that Buddha preached? The keynote of his doctrine was that the earthly life of man was necessarily full of suffering, but that by following the path which he pointed out man could be released from this condition of sorrow. Deliverance from suffering was to be the object of the wise man's efforts. He formulated four sacred truths which treat of suffering. (1.) Earthly life is suffering. (2.) This suffering has a cause; it springs from a thirst for being, from desire, ambition, and lust. (3.) This suffering can be destroyed by expelling and separating oneself from all desire. (4.) And the way to expel desire and thus to extinguish suffering is by acting, and speaking, and thinking righteously. From these primary truths spring all the later doctrines of Buddhism, and all its rules of conduct. The object of each man was to deliver himself from existence and to attain Nirvâna. What Nirvâna exactly means, it is difficult to say. Some have supposed it to mean annihilation, but this doctrine is expressly condemned by Buddhistic writings. Others (amongst them Max Müller) have maintained that Nirvâna is the completion, not the extinction, of being. Oldenberg † holds that exact statements as to the ultimate condition of the perfected saint were carefully evaded, and that the question of the future state was purposely left doubtful. The object of Buddhism was to teach men how to escape from the suffering of the world. It did not care to enlarge on the future condition of those who had escaped.

* Hunter's *Indian Empire*, p. 154. † *Life of Buddha*, p. 281.

From this idea of life there sprang other doctrines. Suffering is always the penalty of a man's actions either in his present or former state of existence. What he sows, that must he inevitably reap. When he dies, he will have to suffer re-birth in a higher or lower state of existence, according to his merit or demerit in the past. The object being to escape from earthly existence, the more merit a man obtains the nearer he is to attaining Nirvâna. From lower to higher conditions of life, through many births and deaths, the man is gradually to extinguish desire and to subdue the cravings of the mind, till at last having become passionless, and complete, and perfected, he will be at peace, absorbed into the Nirvâna, as "the dewdrop slips into the shining sea."

In such a religion as this there was no room for a personal god, no place for sacrifices, no need of temples, no object in prayer. Each man was to be self-delivered. As Gautama Buddha had delivered himself, so each one was to attain deliverance by following the path he pointed out. Knowledge brings salvation; man was to work out his own deliverance, unaided and alone. These doctrines are visible in the two striking series of buildings noticeable in every Buddhistic country, viz.: pagodas and monasteries. The pagodas are not temples. They are erections built over some relic, real or supposed, and are considered sacred because of the memorial which they enshrine. The monasteries are places where those, who wish to obtain merit and to hasten their own deliverance, can retire from the world and live in common, devoting themselves to a celibate and ascetic life, and thus subduing in themselves all earthly desires. These pagodas and monasteries are very striking objects in all parts of Burma, and some description of the chief of them will, I hope, be not without interest.

The great pagoda at Rangoon is called the Shway Dagohn. It is an enormous mass of pyramidal masonry on a circular foundation, which gradually tapers upwards in swelling curves of graceful design till it finally comes to a point 321 feet above the terrace on which it stands. The whole of the surface is smooth, and covered with gold leaf, and when the sun shines upon it, this spire piercing upwards towards the sky glitters from afar. I visited this pagoda on several occasions, and always found objects of interest to attract my attention. The structure itself is built on a flat-topped hill, rising steeply above the town, and it has been strongly fortified. Up this hill there are four long flights of steps, one at each cardinal point, covered by a roof or open arcade made of wood, supported by a double row of pillars. The porches, and beams, and roof ridges, and capitals of the pillars are all richly carved with quaint figures of dragons and monsters. Under this colonnade there is alway a crowd of loungers and sightseers, pilgrims and beggars. There are little stalls on each side, where you can buy offerings to make at the shrine. Up and down the steps pass throngs of men, women, and children, monks with their shaven heads and yellow robes, and sometimes a nun also shaven but dressed in white, looking old and ugly. When the steps are climbed, one comes to a great square platform or terrace, from which the great mass of the pagoda towers upwards.

This pagoda is said to have been erected 2000 years ago over some sacred relics. It is fabled to contain eight hairs of Gautama besides a sacred garment which belonged to an earlier Buddha. It is perfectly solid, and thus does not serve as a temple, (for there is no such thing as a temple in Buddhism,) but it only marks a sacred site. The building assumed its present size and form about a century ago.* One of the most curious parts of the structure is its apex. The masonry finishes in a point, but above that is

* Fergusson, vol. i. p. 52.

placed a metal umbrella-shaped covering made of concentric rings, looking very light in construction and hung with little bells, and said to be inlaid with jewels. This ornament, which is placed on the top of every Burmese pagoda is called a "H'tee," and is a symbol of sovereignty. At the base of the pagoda there are four shrines, facing the four staircases which lead up to the platform. These shrines are full of statues of Gautama, and the pillars and wood-work within and without are very richly carved. They are not entered by the worshippers, and are not very deep, and the images are very visible from the outside. Here offerings are made, candles are burned, and religious formulæ are recited. Every worshipper is expected to make some offering. The poorest bring a handful of flowers or a little rice, or a candle or two. These offerings are deposited before the shrine, and are supposed to earn some merit for the offerer. No one cares what becomes of the offering when made, but if is eatable it is quickly disposed of, as the platform is frequented by pariah dogs, and fowls, and birds, who are never driven away. The spiritual intention of the offerer is the only important thing. If he has offered it with a pure heart, he has gained merit. What happens to the substance of his offering is of no importance. He has done his part by making it, and for that he will gain his due reward.

The statues of Gautama are always made in accordance with one of three conventional designs. The most usual is a sitting figure, but he is also represented as standing, and as reclining. The face bears always a calm and peaceful expression, the lips full, and the mouth closed. The eyes are large and wide apart; the head is covered with ringlets which either represent the hair artificially treated, or are meant to represent some form of close-fitting cap. The lobes of the ears are long and touch the shoulders. The body is generally fully clothed, with the right shoulder and arm bare. The legs are crossed and folded close under the body in an impossible position, with the sole of the left foot turned upwards. The standing figure sometimes has one hand raised in the attitude of blessing. The most striking feature about all these statues is the peaceful expression which the artists have managed to give to the face of Buddha. In spite of a conventionality of treatment and an ignorance of anatomy, they yet have stamped on their images a look of calm happiness and untroubled repose which is very remarkable. Something in these great sitting figures of Gautama reminded me of the monuments in Egypt, where the same unconquerable quietness seemed to be stamped on the statues of the early kings. The more one looked at these figures, the more the thought grew that here was a man who had won rest and peace. The expression was one of great dignity, but far removed from all the strife of earth. The great quiet eyes looked forth in happy meditation, and the serenity of the brows, and the peacefulness of the closed lips, spoke of toil over and Nirvâna attained.

What use the Buddhists make of these figures is not clear. Properly in their religion there is no place for prayer. Man is to be his own deliverer. Gautama has shown them how to live, but he is dead and gone into Nirvâna. A rigid law governs the universe, and a man's circumstances are the outcome of his past actions. There should be no place for prayer, there certainly ought to be no room for idolatry in such a religion as this. Yet man is almost necessarily a praying creature, and it seemed to be allowed that many of the more ignorant Buddhists did look upon Gautama as a god, and made prayers before his images. Ordinarily the worshippers, who looked very devout, and prostrated themselves to the ground before the shrines, were engaged in reciting religious axioms or repeating the rules of life taught by the founder of their religion. But it is said by those who profess to know, that popularly Gautama is looked upon as a god, and addressed in prayer. The ignorant require some visible image, and therefore deify the founder of their religion.

But the great pagoda with its four shrines is not the only thing that stands on the terraced platform. Round it on all sides there are numerous detached buildings, great and small, full of images of Gautama. There are also tall masts decorated with tinsel and bells, draped with cloth, and bright with colour. Great bronze bells hang close to the ground, so that they are within the reach of anyone who desires to strike them, and thus the whole platform is crowded with a number of heterogeneous objects, some of which are substantial and others very impermanent. But the reason why these diverse erections have been placed on the platform is the same in every case. The object has been to obtain merit, and by thus accumulating good deeds to shorten the number of existences which have to be endured before Nirvâna is reached. Thus many wealthy Burmans have enriched the platform of the Shway Dagohn by images of Gautama. Any worshipper may erect what he likes on the platform; the richer puts up a permanent structure, the poorer is content with some slighter offering. But there seems no law to prevent anything being erected, and thus the platform has become crowded with these numerous and diverse objects. Even the bells have their use, for it is a meritorious act to strike them, and by so doing the striker increases the total of his good deeds.

The scene on the platform of the great pagoda is thus curious and picturesque in the extreme. The place is free to all, and is at all hours crowded with sightseers and worshippers. All day long there are offerings being made before the shrines, and even far into the night there are worshippers intoning sacred sentences and prostrating themselves before the sacred spot. Pilgrims come from far to visit this holy site. From Ceylon and Madras, from Siam and

Cambodia, from China and Tibet, and other parts of the world, Buddhists come to see the great Golden Pagoda. At eventide the scene is specially interesting. The pilgrims are numerous. The shrines are always full of offerings, the smaller buildings clustered round are visited in their turn, the deep notes of the bronze bell rise up on the evening air, the great mass of the pagoda towers up, its golden surface turning red in the light of the setting sun, far away are seen the forests of the delta intersected by the great rivers, and as the sun sinks and the light fades from beneath, the lofty H'tee on the summit of the building glows with the ruddy light and shines out as a beacon visible for many miles.

There are quantities of other pagodas scattered over the country, some nearly as large as the Shway Dagohn; indeed the Pegu Pagoda is three feet higher, rising to a height of 324 feet. But every village has its shrine to remind the people of the great teacher. The reason for this multiplication of fanes is obvious. No work of merit is so richly paid as the building of a pagoda. The man who does so is regarded as a saint on earth, and when he dies he obtains the last release. For him there are no more deaths, but he attains the holy rest.* No wonder then that pagodas of all sizes are plentiful in Burma.

The other specially Buddhistic erection is the monastery, called in Burma a Kioung. The primary idea of Buddhism is that earthly existence is an evil, and therefore the main desire of the orthodox Buddhist is to escape from it as soon as possible. And the best way of shortening the term of a man's successive existences is to become a holy monk. From the monastery there is but a short step to Nirvâna. In consequence of this belief there are a number of monasteries in Burma, where he who wishes to lead the higher life of contemplation and self-denial can

* *The Burman*, by Shway Yoe, vol. i. p. 184.

retire from the world, and live the life of a monk. In Burma nearly every boy enters at least for a short time as a novice. He has his head shaved, and he puts on the yellow robe which is the dress of the religious order. But many of the novices return to the world after a short experience of the monastic life. There is no compulsion placed on them to stay; a monk may at any moment become a layman. If he feels unable to live the higher life of contemplation and self-denial, if he desires to marry or to amass wealth, he may leave the Kioung, put off his yellow robe, suffer his hair to grow, and enter into secular business. He knows that by doing so he is preparing for himself a longer sequence of successive existences, but this fear does not deter multitudes from following the secular life. While he is in the world, he is bidden to live according to the precepts of Buddha. And if at any time he becomes disgusted with the outside world, he can retire to the monastery, and be again admitted amongst the "noble order of the yellow robe."

The Kioungs are very noticeable buildings, and have an architectural character of their own. They are groups of detached houses standing together in an enclosure, shaded generally by large and leafy trees. Each house is the abode of one or more monks, and all are marked by the number of their roofs placed one above the other. These roofs overlap each other, and the eaves, and ridges, and gables, are very richly carved. These roof ridges mark the Kioung, and denote its sacred character. Generally the basement story is open and not used as a living room. Above that is the main part of the house, which is reached by an outside stair-case which opens on to a verandah running round the building. From this covered balcony the various rooms open out. Dr. Marks, the well-known S.P.G. missionary in Rangoon, took me to visit one of the houses in a Kioung inhabited by the Prior. As soon as we entered the precincts, we were rushed at by a quantity of pariah dogs, who are always loitering about the monastic buildings. They act as watch-dogs at night, and would prevent any stranger from approaching the building unheard. They were large savage-looking beasts, but if well pelted with sticks and stones they did not approach very near, but kept up a continual barking from a distance. Ascending the stair-case of the central building, we found the head monk sitting at the door of the room, chewing betel. He was not an agreeable looking person, as he was old, toothless, and dirty, and his habit of chewing betel made him expectorate a good deal of red saliva. We approached him with great respect, and when we sat down on the floor to talk with him, we were careful to tuck our feet as much out of sight as possible. In Burma it is never polite to sit with the feet obtruded, and in interviews with royalty they should never be exhibited at all. It is said that those Englishmen who are permitted to have the honour of a conversation with his Majesty King Thebaw at Mandalay undergo severe tortures from the cramped position which it is necessary to assume, Court etiquette requiring them to sit on their feet, and thus conceal them from view. After Dr. Marks had conversed with the Prior, he showed us some of the treasures of the monastery. We saw some beautiful sacred books, made of palm leaves which were lacquered over, and the letters, also of lacquer, were inlaid in different colours. The central room was full of presents, which had been presented to the monks by the faithful laity. Many of these were English goods, such as moderator lamps and hearth-rugs. There were also images of Gautama, and parts of the central room could be partitioned off, thus making sleeping rooms for monks and novices. Within the precincts of the monastery there is always a school for boys, who are taught by the monks. This system of monastic schools covers the whole country, and in consequence nearly every Burmese boy knows how to read and write. Though the education given is meagre, it is better than nothing, and these monastic schools are attended by all classes of the community.

The life of a monk (or "Pohngyee" as he is called in Burma) is spent in contemplation and prayer. His chief work is to learn to recite the sacred books, and to teach them to the pupils who attend the school. He lives solely on the offerings of the laity, and is not allowed to possess any property. His sole garment is a yellow robe, his only chattel a begging bowl. Latterly the monasteries have become possessed of certain goods, which have been presented to them by the laity, but these are not the property of individuals, but belong to the corporate body of monks. Since their only way of obtaining food is by begging, it will be seen that the chief work of the day must be to collect the offerings of the faithful. Each morning about eight o'clock* a long procession of monks sallies forth in Indian file, each bearing a bowl. They wend their way through the principal streets, but they never stop to ask for anything. Their eyes should be fixed steadfastly on the ground, their minds should be full of thoughts of their own unworthiness and of the vileness of all earthly things. For the chief motive of the daily begging round is not (as might be supposed) to obtain supplies for the monastery, but to afford an opportunity to the laity to obtain merit by alms-giving. It is not for their own sakes, but for the sake of the givers that the monks thus make their round. Therefore they neither ask for anything, nor utter any word of thanks when something is placed in their bowls. The gifts benefit the giver more than the receiver. To feed a holy monk is to do a meretorious action. The man or woman who thus gets an opportunity of acquiring merit is the one who ought to be grateful. The monk is merely giving them a chance of showing their obedience to the commands of Buddha. Thus if the bowls are filled before the

* See *The Burman*, by Shway Yoe.

round is completed, they are emptied by the roadside. This food is devoured by dogs or birds, and so is not wasted, and thus room is made for more offerings. The opportunity of giving is presented to all, so that none may lose the chance of accumulating merit. Thus the monk does not feel that he is degraded by living on charity. Rather is he a recipient of gifts which do more good to the givers than to himself.

The daily begging round is not the only way in which the monasteries benefit from the custom of alms-giving. Every Burman considers it a privilege to be allowed to minister to a Pohngyee's wants, and thus the Pohngyees receive numerous gifts. A rich layman at certain seasons of the year will make up a large quantity of useful gifts, and send them with great pomp to the Kioung. He is by no means careful to conceal his charitable offerings, "but sounds a trumpet in the streets" that "he may have glory of men." I saw such an offering on its way through the town going to the monastery. First came a band of music, playing discordant tunes, to attract the attention of the bystanders. Then followed a line of coolies bearing gifts. There must have been fifty of them, and they formed quite a long procession. The presents were very various; plates, lamps, rugs, cloth, cushions, towels, tea cups, crockery, all arranged in pretty erections on bamboo frames, gaily decorated with streamers and flowers, almost in the shape of Christmas-trees. These were all to be carried to some Kioung for the benefit of the Pohngyees.

It is difficult to estimate the spiritual effect which a strange religion has on its adherents, and yet some effort ought to be made to guess at the effect which Buddhism produces in Burma. The good points of the religion are evident. It encourages kindliness and humanity, it denounces idolatry, it enforces charity and good works by the strongest motives of self-interest. But with these good points there are other doctrines and practices which are less praiseworthy. Buddhism is essentially a pessimistic religion. Its fundamental doctrine is that human life is an evil, from which escape is necessary. Hence the world is looked upon as full of sorrow and suffering where happiness is unattainable. This leads to a contempt for all human affections, and a disinclination to take part in the affairs of life. From this springs the exaltation of the monastic idea, which insists on the superior holiness of the celibate and ascetic life. And this leads to two standards of holiness, one for the monk and the other for the laity, and certain practices are forbidden as sinful in the one, and yet are permitted as harmless in the other. The whole of common life is thus degraded, and its duties are neglected and despised, because those, who are considered the holiest, think it necessary to come out from the world and live apart. Chistianity purifies and sanctifies all human relationships, and earthly duties. In Buddhism the ideal life is lived in the cloister apart from the world. The antagonism between the two religions is fundamental, for while Buddhism looks on earthly existence as an evil, Chistianity bids us use it as a training ground, where we are being educated for something higher.

The fatalism of Buddhism must not be overlooked. The gods themselves are subject to an unbending law; the future is determined by the past, and forgiveness is as impossible as a miracle. This teaching has a great charm for many minds. They are glad to hear a stern enforcement of the truth (common to Christianity as well as to Buddhism) that "whatsoever a man soweth, that shall he also reap." But while both religions insist on the doctrine of retribution, and that the consequences of all our actions follow by a necessary law, yet Christianity tells us also of a possibility of renewal, and how God Who punishes us also desires that the punishment may lead us nearer to Himself. Buddhism holds out no hope to the sinner, only the revenge of an outraged law falling in merciless severity on the transgressor. Christianity insists equally on the fact that we have to bear the consequences of our own actions, but it also tells us of a loving Father, Who is ever striving to guide and influence the wills of men. In the one religion nothing but the law is insisted upon; in the other we are bidden to see behind the law the face of God as revealed by Christ.

There is one more point of difference between Christianity and Buddhism which is noticeable, and that is the way in which each thinks of its founder. Each religion holds up the life of its founder as an example to be followed, each professes to be guided by the doctrines he preached. But Buddhism treats Gautama Buddha as no longer alive; he once lived, but is now in Nirvâna. Christianity on the other hand bids us trust evermore in a living Lord, with Whom each believer has a real communion and intercourse. Buddhism leaves each man to be the author of his own deliverance, and offers him an example of conduct and certain rules of life as his only aid on the upward path. The elementary conception of Christianity involves a living relation with One "Who died and is alive again." The example of the holiest life and the enunciation of the purest rules of conduct can do but little to restrain the passions and vivify the will. It needs besides a present help from a living Lord, and this is the fundamental doctrine of Christianity. Buddhism has become practically Atheism, and its closest followers consider that they have won their position by their own exertions. This makes them proud and self-satisfied, inclined to look down on the common people who know not the law. The Christian admits that he owes all his righteousness to the continual presence of his indwelling Lord, and he would be the first to allow that he can only do all things through Christ Who strengtheneth him.

I have drawn out this comparison between the two

religions, because I found so many Christians living in Buddhistic countries who were to my mind unduly complimentary to Buddhism. They seemed to me to praise it rightly, when they spoke of its teaching of retribution, and how a man's past affects his future life even on earth. They did not seem to me always to remember that this is a part of Christian teaching also.

They also praised the doctrine of alms-giving, and observed how rightly the followers of Buddha considered the opportunity of giving rather as a privilege to the giver than as a reason for gratitude on the part of the recipient. They did not always remember that this was likewise Christian doctrine, and that our Lord said that it was more blessed to give than to receive. Mixed up with the charity of the Buddhists there is also the doctrine of merit, which to my mind spoils the beauty of the offering, since the giver's main object is the receiving of a reward.

I think the beauty of Buddha's teaching has also been exaggerated. Undoubtedly he was a wonderful person, far in advance of his countrymen. His influence has also lasted, and his disciples are very numerous. But there were contemporaries of his perhaps equally great, and the beauty of Isaiah's writing seems to me more striking than the passages I have seen translated from the recorded words of Buddha.

It is possible to admire the good points of Buddhism without denying the superiority of Christianity. Buddhism was an immense advance on Brahmanism, and gave a death-blow to a large amount of idolatry. But it made its followers proud and self-sufficient, and led directly to practical Atheism. Its best doctrines are, I think, contained in Christianity, and that religion seems to hold up a nobler ideal of life, and also shows its professors the way in which they may reach a higher standard of holiness.

Chapter VII.

In the last chapter I have tried to compare Buddhism with Christianity. The missionaries of the latter religion are trying to exhibit its superiority to the natives of Burma, and I must not omit to mention their efforts and their success. In a country so devoted to education as Burma the missionaries wisely throw much of their strength into school work. The people are accustomed to see their own Pohngyees acting as schoolmasters, they value education, and there is a native school in every village connected with the monastery. Thus the first idea of missions in Burma was educational, and they have borne this character ever since. The missionaries have opened schools in every town and village which they have occupied, and through these schools they have been able to do much to influence the young. With this scheme of evangelization through education the name of the Rev. Dr. Marks, S.P.G. missionary at Rangoon, will ever be connected. Dr. Marks has laboured in Burma for more than twenty years, and his fame as a Christian schoolmaster spread even beyond the bounds of British Burma. In 1863 the then King of Burma invited Dr. Marks to come to his capital at Mandalay, and there offered to build a church and school at his own expense, and to send some of his own sons to be educated. The present King Thebaw was one of Dr. Marks's pupils, and for a time the school at Mandalay was in a flourishing condition. A church was built and consecrated, and there seemed every prospect of a permanent mission being established at the capital. But the King's caprice did not last, the school languished, and when King Thebaw came to the throne in 1878, and signalized his accession by murdering all his relations, the mission was withdrawn. The original reason for the late King's invitation was chiefly political. He wished to gain credit with the English, and he hoped to induce Dr. Marks to act as his intermediary, and to obtain through him certain concessions from the Government of India. When the late King found that he could not make the missionary his tool, he quickly withdrew his countenance from the school, which he had seemed at one time so ready to favour.

But though the mission has been forced to withdraw from Independent Burma its work in British Burma is increasing on every side. The school and orphanage which Dr. Marks has founded in Rangoon are the most successful institutions of their kind in the Province. S. John's College, as it is called, consists of a number of detached buildings, built of teak, standing in a compound. Here are schools and dormitories, residences for the masters, a play-ground for the lads, class-rooms and dining halls, all large and airy, capable of accommodating several hundred boys. In the middle is the chapel, also of teak, bright with colour and handsomely decorated. The school is open to boys of any religion or any nationality. Some come as day boys, others as boarders. The number on the books when I was there was 434, comprising 61 Europeans and Anglo-Burmese, 258 Burmese, 72 Chinese, and 43 natives of India. Christianity forms a part of the school curriculum. The parents know that this is the case, so if heathens send their children to the school, they do it with their eyes open. A Bible lesson is given each day to the whole school, and there are daily prayers, but the heathen boys only listen without joining in them. The orphanage is confined to boys whose fathers are dead, and these are all baptized. The school is divided into three divisions: the High, the Middle, and the Primary, and in time it is hoped that some of the highest class may pass the matriculation examination of the Calcutta University. It was a pleasant sight to see how the lads played and worked together, the different nationalities apparently in perfect harmony. They all could talk Burmese, and all learned English. There was no difficulty in most cases about food or caste prejudices, as all (except the natives of India) were willing to eat together. Boys came as boarders often from long distances, and though at first they were often rough in manner and shy, yet soon the discipline and happy life of the school won them over to quieter manners and friendly relationships with all. Dr. Marks seemed to be known and loved by them all, and his study was always open to those who had requests to make, or questions to ask. About 10 per cent. are converted to Christianity during their school course, but the indirect effect of the teaching they here receive should also be considered. The Christians, who have left school and gone into various occupations, do well; they are pastorally visited by the missionaries, and many come on Sundays to the school chapel, liking to take part in the services to which they have been accustomed.

On Christmas-Day I was invited to attend the service in the chapel, and to preach to the congregation. The building consisted of a central nave, with side compartments which could be shut off with folding doors. The centre was reserved for the Christian congregation, which consisted of the scholars who had been baptized, the "old boys" and their wives, and any native Christians who liked to attend. But the side compartments, which were not really part of the chapel, were open to all. They served the purpose of side aisles, and their occupants could see and hear all that was going on. These side rooms could also be freely entered from the street outside, so that any passer-by could stand and listen to the service, and leave again at pleasure. Whilst the service was going on, I saw a Pohngyee in his yellow robe and with his head shaved enter, and watch, and listen for a time, but he soon left. The heathen boys belonging to the school sat in these side compartments. The chapel was prettily decorated with texts, and flowering creepers, the Burmese ladies were dressed in their brightest coloured silks, and everything was in festal attire. The service was fully choral, and in English, except the lessons, which were in Burmese. My sermon was translated sentence by sentence as I delivered it. It was a little difficult at first to compose in detached fragments. Each sentence had as far as possible to be a complete thought, and I had to retain the thread of the discourse while Dr. Marks was interpreting the last sentence. After the sermon was over, the heathen lads were dismissed, the doors opening from the side compartments were shut, and then in the presence of the Christians only the Holy Communion was celebrated. The service was in English, but the words of administration were said in Burmese. Several Chinese Christians communicated, wearing their native dress, and having pigtails reaching below their knees. Altogether it was a most interesting service, and I was glad to have had the opportunity of joining in it.

After service there were various Christmas gifts to be distributed. The Burmese ladies (wives of old scholars) had brought tarts for the orphans; every boy got something, and at 4 o'clock in the afternoon they were to have a big Christmas dinner. A sad incident had happened on the previous day, which cast a gloom over the Christmas festivities. While Dr. Marks and the Christian boys had been attending a service at the pro-Cathedral, two of the heathen boys, who had been left behind in the school, had begun quarrelling, and one had stabbed the other with a pocket-knife. Thus while the Christmas services were going on, one boy was lying in a very critical condition in the hospital, while another was locked up in jail. The fight arose from some boyish quarrel. The Burmans are very irascible and the blow was struck in a moment, and nearly proved fatal. The stabber was a prince of the royal house of

Mandalay, who had had to flee from King Thebaw, as his father had been filled with gunpowder by the King's orders, and then exploded.

Besides the mission at Rangoon there are many other centres of work in various parts of Burma. The general feeling amongst those missionaries whom I saw was hopeful: there is none of the difficulty of caste which is found amongst the Hindus in India, but the people are willing to give their confidence to the missionaries, and admit them into their houses. Buddhism, though a difficult religion to combat, has yet points which touch Christianity. It is possible to argue from the basis of a common morality and converts are led to own the superiority of Christ to Buddha. The women and children are more easily influenced than those of India, and the future of missions in Burma seemed hopeful. Even amongst the Karens, who are the wild tribes of the interior, much has been done. These people are of a lower type than the Burmese, and profess a system of devil worship. They have responded very warmly to the efforts which have been made for them, and numbers have become Christians. The missions in Burma have seemed to take a fresh start since 1877, when the Province was made a separate diocese. The present Bishop of Rangoon, Dr. Strahan, was formerly a missionary in Tinnevelly. He has spiritual jurisdiction over both the Government chaplains and the missionaries, but his sympathies seem specially keen towards those labouring amongst the heathen. He is the first of those sent out from S. Augustine's Missionary College at Canterbury who has been consecrated a Bishop, and all old S. Augustine's boys have rejoiced at his preferment.

After spending some days at Rangoon, I visited some of the other towns in Burma. I went by rail to Prome, which is up the Irrawaddy 163 miles due north of Rangoon. It is the terminus of the only railway at present completed in Burma. We made the journey by night, and so saw but little of the intervening country. It is chiefly jungle, with clearings of cultivated ground round the villages, in which paddy is grown. The soil seemed very rich, and in some of the gardens near Rangoon we saw fields of pine apples growing like potatoes at home. Prome itself is prettily situated on the bank of the Irrawaddy, which here flows underneath a range of low hills which are well wooded, and many of them crowned with small pagodas. From Prome you can steam up the river to Mandalay, King Thebaw's capital, and even to Bhamô, a town on the frontiers of China. Large steamers drawing only four feet of water ascend the river, towing large flats filled with all sorts of merchandise. There is a great traffic with the interior, and the Irrawaddy is the chief means by which the country has been opened up for trade. Mandalay is about 250 miles from Prome, and Bhamô is 200 miles farther up the river. We heard many stories of the cruelty and debaucheries of the King, and how badly he governed the country. He encourages lotteries as a means of raising revenue, and he also grants monopolies to those who will bid the highest sum, or succeed in bribing his ministers. There are Englishmen and Italians who have managed to secure such monopolies by giving presents to the King, and who are thus able to make fortunes at the expense of the people of the country. Every interview with this monarch has to be purchased by presents, and the bribery and corruption in his Court are excessive. His army is composed of a mass of undrilled and badly-armed men, who could be easily overthrown by disciplined troops. Many of the merchants in British Burma desire that the English should annex Thebaw's dominions. They say that the country would pay for annexation, and that the introduction of good government would be a benefit to the inhabitants. Certainly there would be no military difficulty in the operation, and no doubt the dwellers in Upper Burma would share in the prosperity of their brethren within our borders. But apart from the moral question as to our right to annex Thebaw's dominions, there is also the diplomatic consideration, whether it would be wise to let our frontier touch that of China. It would add to the military precautions we have to take, for if we had a strong and thickly populated nation like China on our border, instead of a weak and sparse people as at present, we should require to keep a larger number of troops in the country. There is already a considerable trade with China by means of the Irrawaddy, and it is hoped that better trade routes will soon be discovered. Bhamô is the highest point to which steamers at present ascend, and from there overland roads lead into southern and western China. Many attempts have been made to explore and open out this country, one of the last expeditions being that of Mr. Colquhoun, who has told in his book, *Across Chrysê*, how he travelled from Canton to Bhamô.

All this was discussed, as we journeyed to Prome, and stood on the bank of the Irrawaddy. I had neither time nor opportunity to penetrate further into the interior, but I could not help letting my imagination follow the course of the great river, and wish that I could journey up its waters, and see the wonders of Mandalay, and the Chinese frontier at Bhamô. But I had to be satisfied with Prome itself, as the longer journey would have taken several weeks to accomplish.

The great feature of Prome itself is the pagoda, which is well situated on a high hill. It is not so high as the Shway Dagohn, but the ascent is steeper, and the arcade more richly carved. The view from the platform was most extensive, over a wide expanse of well wooded country, with long reaches of the river to the north and to the south. We walked through the bazaar, which was full of English goods, cottons, and hardware of all sorts. The native manufactures were chiefly lacquer and brass work. There were also stalls for fruit and vegetables, and great masses of "nga-pee" or fish-paste. This fish-paste is considered a great delicacy by the Burmese, but it is not pleasing to an Englishman's olfactory nerves. It is composed of more or less decayed fish, pounded into a paste and mixed with salt. This is eaten as a relish with rice, but as the composition is often rather "high," the smell of it is enough for most Europeans. The most delicate is made from pounded prawns, but the commoner sorts are composed of all sorts of fishes mashed together. If a steamer gets to leeward of a boat laden with these delicacies, the passengers hold their noses, and request the captain to proceed as quickly as possible.

Besides visiting Prome I also went to Moulmein. This is a town near the coast about 150 miles to the south-east of Rangoon. Our steamer was a fast one, and we did the distance in about eleven hours. For the greater part of the day we were out of sight of land, as we had to cross a deep bay, but the last part of the voyage was up the Salween river, on which the town is situated. This part of the trip was most beautiful, as the river banks were clothed with cocoa-nut trees and other palms, and the evening light on the wooded banks was most lovely. Moulmein itself is situated a few miles up the Salween river, which is here about a quarter of a mile wide. The houses are built on piles, and stand amongst groves of cocoa-nut and jack-fruit trees, and look most picturesque from the water. Behind the town, which extends for more than a mile along the river bank, there is a ridge of hills parallel to the river, along which there are numerous pagodas built on the commanding heights; this ridge made a most beautiful background to the scene, all glowing as it was in the evening light.

On the next day we had a splendid drive all along this ridge, and I saw some of the prettiest scenery I had seen in my travels. On the other side of the ridge there is another river called the Atteran, and this joins the Salween just above Moulmein. Thus looking down from the ridge we saw miles of country well wooded and fertile, we could trace the great rivers winding for miles, and the hills and plains, the woods and waters, made a lovely view. Below us there were great ships lying anchored in the stream, the roofs of the houses peeped out amongst groves of cocoa-nuts, small canoes hollowed out of teak-logs were being paddled about in all directions, and crowds of gaily dressed natives filled all the streets. We noticed some curious limestone rocks which rose up very steeply and abruptly from the plain about five miles distant, and these we visited next morning to see some famous caves.

These caves are natural recesses in the limestone, and have been made into shrines to hold images of Gautama. The first we entered was quite full of statues, of all sizes and in all positions. Some were only a few feet high, while others were colossal. Some of the reclining figures were 30 to 40 feet in length, made of brick work, covered with plaster, and placed in natural niches in the living rock. Many had been gilded over with gold leaf, and were ornamented with bits of glittering mica and glass. All had, however, been shamefully mutilated, hardly one having escaped the wanton mischief of former visitors. Names had been scribbled everywhere, the heads and hands of the images knocked off, and often whole figures removed. There seems no one to take any care of these interesting figures, nor to check the Vandalism of tourists. This first cave is not very deep, but it runs along the face of the rock like a gallery, and is about 60 yards long, 6 yards wide, and about 20 feet high.

There is a second cave which is much larger, and has been left in its natural state. It is entered by a narrow orifice, and is the abode of countless numbers of bats, who were awakened and disturbed by our entrance. We carried torches, and in certain places we burnt blue lights, to show us the great size of the cavern. It opened out into large and lofty chambers, the roof often being 50 feet above our heads, and there were several passages branching out from the various chambers in different directions. Long stalactites hung from the roof, and formed grotesque pillars, and the floor was thickly covered with bats' guano. We must have been half-an-hour scrambling about the various passages of this enormous cave.

We visited the great timber yards at Moulmein, where the teak is prepared for exportation. This is one of the chief articles of trade from this port. The trees are cut in Siam by native contractors, and the logs are dragged by trained elephants through the jungle to the nearest stream or water-course. During the rainy season these logs are floated down the streams, and are joined together into large rafts, which finally arrive at Moulmein, where they are bought by the timber merchants. Their yards are built along the side of the river, and here the logs are landed, squared and stacked, ready for shipment to England or elsewhere. All the heavy work inside the yard is done by trained elephants, and it is their clever labour, which makes the sight so curious and interesting. They drag the logs on to the land, they place them in the saw-shed to be squared, they drag them from thence to the stacking-place, and then stack them up into large rectangular heaps. Several of the elephants were brought out for our inspection, and the docility and sagacity of these great beasts were marvellous. The creature seemed to understand exactly what was required from him. The mahout, who rode on his neck, directed him by voice or touch, and the elephant obeyed each direction as it was given. Even when the mahout purposely dropped the iron hook with which an elephant is driven, the creature picked it off the ground with his trunk, and meekly handed it back to the man who had thus obtained dominion over him. We saw an elephant pushing large logs along the ground, which weighed between one and two tons; he seemed to kick them forward with the greatest ease, with a flip of one of his large feet. He also rolled the log over at the word of command, so as to exhibit each side in turn, and then lifted it on to the stack. This last operation was the most curious of all. The elephant knelt down, and got his tusks under the end of the log, which was lying nearest to the stack. Then he put his trunk over it to steady it, and standing up he raised that end on to the pile, which was about six feet high. He then went to the other end of the log and pushed it along first with his trunk, and afterwards (as the end of the log rose up) with his head, till the log lay on the stack exactly square with the others.

We were told that an untrained elephant cost about 1000 rupees, and when trained it was worth about 2500. The animal comes to maturity at about 20 years old, and can then be worked. It learns to be of some use in a few months, and goes on working as long as it lives. The oldest we saw was about 60, but they live to 75 years. When they first enter the timber yards, they are not quite wild, as they have generally been used by native contractors to haul logs in the forests. They have, however, to be taught to stand the noise of the steam whistle and the saw machinery, but they soon get accustomed to the constant whirr and hum of the engines, and by degrees they pick up their finer accomplishments. The common idea that the elephant does not breed in captivity is a vulgar error. Most of the elephants used in the yards are bred by native foresters, who use them for hauling purposes, and then sell them to the timber merchants. It does not pay European firms, or the Government, to breed elephants, as they have to be kept so long before becoming useful. They are therefore bought from the native foresters, who breed them from their herds in the forest, where the young ones pick up a living at no expense.

The elephant when working is an expensive animal to feed, for he daily eats 100 bundles of grass and 75 lbs. of paddy. A syce or groom is attached to each elephant, and he gives him his food. Their stables are high sheds, which shelter them from the heat and wet, and they are confined by chains put round their feet. The animal is so docile that he will chain himself up at the word of command, passing the links round his foot with his trunk. The chain is then secured with a padlock for fear lest he should be as clever in unloosing himself when he is left alone. Before being tied up for the night each elephant is allowed to enter the river for a bath. This seemed to be much enjoyed, and the huge beasts sank their whole bodies under the water, leaving only the tips of their trunks exposed. The mahouts had to stand upright on their backs, and were then in water up to their knees. This was the treat given to them at the end of the day's work, and seemed to be much appreciated. We were told that the elephants learn to recognize the steam whistle which gives the signal for stopping work and for the mid-day meal; and there is one old elephant who will no more work after that has sounded, than a farm labourer will go on after the bell has rung. If they want to get extra work out of him, they have to deceive him by ordering the whistle not to be sounded. The mahouts seemed to have the most perfect command over the huge creatures, and made them do whatever they were told. Sometimes an elephant will become dangerous for a time, and then if he is loose, he will "take charge of the yard," for until he is secured, none can enter through the gates. However, they are watched very carefully, and as soon as any dangerous symptoms are seen, the animal is confined and dieted till the fit has passed. The whole timber trade of Burma is made possible by the docility and sagacity of the elephant, for if it were not for him, the expense of labour and machinery would absorb all the profits.

From Moulmein we went back to Rangoon, and from there started on another expedition to Pegu. This city is the old capital of the Talaings. The Talaings and Burmans were the two races who in ancient days divided the country between them. They were both descended from a Tibetan stock, and overran the country in successive invasions. In the earliest historical notices of Burma the Talaings held the coast, and the Burmans had the interior of the country. There were constant wars and fightings between the two peoples, until in the last century the Burmans conquered the Talaings and almost exterminated them. There are very few pure Talaings left, and their language is rapidly dying out, but the two nations have intermingled to some extent.

Pegu itself is a town about 54 miles from Rangoon up the Pegu river, which is a tributary of the Irrawaddy, and joins it just below Rangoon. We made our expedition in a steam launch, and had rather an exciting journey. We started at 2 p.m., when the tide was nearly at its lowest, and we made good progress up the river as the tide flowed. It was a broad stream, half-a-mile in width, but shallow and full of sand banks. As we travelled up the stream, the throb of our engines was the only sound we heard. It was a desolate-looking river. Now and then we saw a fisherman, watching his nets; occasionally we passed a few houses scattered on the bank, from which the children stared at us. But the greater part of our voyage was between flat banks from which the paddy had been reaped. The water swarmed with fish, and there were quantities of stake and drift-nets set across the current, which were watched by native fishermen in canoes dug out of teak logs. The Burman is very fond of fish of all kinds, and has invented various traps made of bamboo, which are set in the tideways of the rivers. These are on the principle of the English eel basket, into which the fish can easily enter, but then fail to discover the way out.

After four hours of this monotonous voyage the sun set, and we were still many miles from Pegu. Our Mohammedan engine-driver said his prayers on the deck-roof of the cabin, undisturbed by the propinquity of those who were unbelievers. There were seven of us altogether in the launch (two English and five natives), and our boat kept puffing onwards, making fair progress up the stream. There was no twilight. The stars rushed out overhead and "with one stride came the dark;" and there we were, travelling onwards up the lonely river, with barely light enough to avoid the fishing-boats which we overtook.

About 8 p.m. the river got shallower, and the tide began to ebb. It was very dark, and there was no possibility of seeing where the deepest channel lay. The result was that we found ourselves constantly running on to sand banks, and were brought up short by sticking in the mud. However there were no rocks or stones, and we always managed to cut through or to back off the obstruction. We must have touched ground some eight or ten times in the next two hours, and we often heeled over a good deal, but fortunately without being swamped. About 10 p.m. we got to the mouth of the canal, which connects the Pegu with the Sattang river. Here we were told that the Pegu river, on which we were, was too shallow for the launch to proceed further, and that it would be wiser for us to steam up the canal about eight miles, and then stop at a village on the bank which would be only seven miles distant by road from Pegu. This we determined to do. So we waited at the mouth of the canal till 11 p.m., when the moon rose, and then by her light we got through the lock and steamed slowly up the canal, till we reached the village about 1 a.m. There we found a carriage sent to meet us, and next morning we drove into Pegu.

The chief sight of this town (which we had found it so

difficult to reach) was the great pagoda, 324 feet high. This is the most lofty one in the province, and is famous for having had a new "H'tee," or umbrella, placed on its apex about a year ago. This H'tee was a very bright one, being made of gilded metal and inlaid with jewels. The successive concentric rings were arranged in a pyramidal form, and the open metal work designs were very light and tasteful. The top was ornamented with a gilt flag, and the whole was hung with bells. We were shown the old H'tee, which had been taken down when the new one was put up, and were surprised at its size. The immense height of the pagoda makes it difficult to realise how large the metal umbrella is, which is fixed on the top. But the remains of the old one enabled us to perceive that the H'tee must be 20 feet high, and 12 feet in diameter at the base. To give a new H'tee to a pagoda is a very meritorious action, and gains great religious credit for the donor. The hoisting up of this metal erection to the top of a smooth spire was a great engineering feat, which the Burmans successfully accomplished without European assistance.

Besides this great pagoda, we were shown a brazen image of Gautama, which stands in a shrine within the precincts of a Kioung or monastery. This image has only been lately set up by a Burman, who is in Government employ. A curious scene took place at the casting of the image. When the image was being finished, it was discovered that there was not sufficient molten metal to fill the mould. This was at once announced to the crowds who had assembled to see the sight, and offerings were demanded from those present. Immediately women stripped off their bangles and jewels and ornaments, men presented silver coins to be melted down, and thus sufficient metal was obtained by these voluntary offerings to complete the image. All the donors would feel that they had earned merit by their gifts, and had helped to perfect a good action.

While we were at Pegu, we heard many stories of the disturbed condition of the country. All Burma is infested with robbers, but latterly armed bands had been scouring the Pegu district committing robberies on travellers. These "dacoits," as they are called, lie in wait on the river banks for people returning from the towns with the money they had received from the sale of their "paddy." The robbers are generally armed, and the country people have little chance in making any resistance. The thick jungle, which covers most of the country, affords them ample hiding-place, and the police find it very difficult to break up the bands or track them to their lairs.

We returned to Rangoon by the same route, and had an equally difficult journey. The river seemed full of sand banks, and though the stream was a quarter of a mile wide, the navigable channel was very narrow. Our launch drew only a few feet of water, but yet we touched the ground very often, and we stuck on one bank for nearly four hours. Fortunately we were well provisioned, and the cook produced a capital dinner. Our only contretemps was a sudden heel over of the launch, for as the tide fell the boat suddenly settled down on one side, with the result that our milk jug was upset, some crockery went overboard, and one rifle sank to the bottom and was never recovered. However, when the tide rose, we floated off the bank, and managed to get back into the right channel, and arrived at Rangoon at 1 a.m. on the morning of January 2nd, 1883.

This was my last expedition in Burma, and on the 4th I started for Southern India. I was very glad to have had this glimpse of Burma, and I would recommend everyone who is touring in our Eastern possessions not to omit paying a visit to Rangoon. The scenery of Burma looks so luxuriant after the bare plains of Northern India, the people are so bright and interesting, the pagodas so graceful, and the whole aspect of the place so full of tropicial colour and diverse life. The gaily dressed crowds fill every town with interest, and the thick trees and noble rivers and tangled jungle make the country districts well worth a visit. Here also Buddhism can be studied under one of its most pleasing forms, for it here bears a less superstitious shape than it does either in China or Ceylon. Besides all these points of interest, Burma is especially interesting to the politician. Here the "Expansion of England" is still at work, and a province over which we have ruled for less than thirty-five years is seen in the process of being brought into order. When it is remembered for how short a time the English have been masters of the country, everyone must be astonished at the signs of prosperity and the rapid progress visible on every side. Much remains to be done, but the amount of good work already accomplished, and the evident popularity of our rule reflect great credit on the hard-working civilians and officers, who have so well administered the country.

My voyage back to India was by a line of steamers, plying from Rangoon to Madras. They do not go direct to Madras, but touch on their way at several of the ports on the eastern coast of India. We were four days crossing the Bay of Bengal, and then made the Indian coast at a small place called Calingapatam. These four days were very quiet and uneventful. We had very few European passengers on board, but the fore part of the vessel was crowded with coolies, returning to their Indian homes after having saved money in Burma. These coolies are employed as labourers in the rice factories, and as porters on the wharves, and get higher pay than they do in India. This causes a great movement of labour between India and Burma, as after a few years' labour a coolie can return, having saved a small fortune. We had about 600 coolies on board, bound for the different ports at which we were to touch. One died while we were at sea, and the Captain had to take charge of his effects, and to deliver them to the nearest relations.

Each night after sunset we had a vivid view of the zodiacal light, which was very brilliant, extending up to the zenith, and shining for many hours. The light is said to proceed from countless myriads of meteoric bodies surrounding the sun, which reflect the sunlight long after the sun itself has sunk below the horizon.

Calingapatam, where we first cast anchor, seemed a small place as viewed from the sea. It is built along the beach, with no bay or port to give shelter to ships. All along this eastern coast of India there are no good harbours, and a constant surf breaks along the shore, which makes landing difficult even on the calmest days. Our steamer was obliged to anchor a mile from the land, and the passengers and cargo were landed in large Masula boats. These boats are of native make, and are rowed by a dozen or more men, often two or three working at one oar. Besides these large boats, we were also visited by catamarans. These are simply two or three logs tied together, on which one or two nearly naked natives crouch, and paddle themselves through the surf. These rafts carry no cargo, but come out in the roughest weather, and live in any sea. The logs are unsinkable, and the crew have no clothes to get spoilt by the sea. The Masula boats brought out to us hides and rice, which seemed the chief exports of the place. We lay all day long off this port, anchored outside the surf, but exposed to a heavy swell, under a hot sun, and the long roll and heave of the vessel was trying to anyone subject to seasickness. In the evening we started for Bimlipatam, our next stopping place, about fifty miles farther down the coast.

We arrived there about 6 a.m., and I landed in a Masula boat, and had a few hours on shore. The station was small, but prettily situated, being built on the edge of the sea under a high hill. The chief trade of the place was in grain, rice, and oil nuts. The voyage through the surf, both going and returning, was a new experience. As we neared the shore the rowers laboured harder at the oars, the steersman kept the boat's head straight, the big waves lifted and bumped us into shallower and shallower water, and at last we grounded on the sandy beach, and were carried in chairs by our bare-legged crew on to dry ground. The wood-work of these boats is tied together with cocoa-nut fibre, and they resist a great amount of knocking about without going to pieces. Where the planks of an English-made boat would be separated, and every nail started, and the boats wrecked, these native-made boats bump about and are none the worse.

From Bimlipatam we went to Vizagapatam, two hours farther down the coast. Here there is a deep creek running inland, which may become the future port of this part of India. At present there is an awkward bar and sunken rocks, but if these could be removed, the place might be made a harbour of refuge from the destructive cyclones.

All along this coast there is a large manufacture of salt, made from the sea-water by evaporation. As salt is very heavily taxed, and as the manufacture of salt is a monopoly, this coast has to be very carefully watched to prevent the Government being defrauded by illegitimate manufacture. I heard some interesting statistics on this subject. The salt tax is the only tax which affects the ryot or peasant of India, but when people first hear that this tax is placed on a necessary of life, that it raises the value of the commodity a thousand per cent., and that illicit manufacture is very severely punished, they think that this must be a crying abuse, which ought to be abolished. But further information often softens the anger of the philanthropic reformer. This tax brings in seven millions a year to the revenue, and is the only tax paid by the very poor, and it amounts to only eightpence a head per annum on the whole population. It would be difficult to obtain so large an amount by any better system, and in return for this small contribution the natives enjoy perfect security and good government. This revenue is collected by raising the price of salt to the consumer. The total cost of manufacture is about 6¼d. a maund (*i. e.*, 82⅐lbs.), and the price charged to the consumer is 5s. a maund, the balance being net profit. The Government at present manufacture most of the salt which is made, but anyone is allowed to make it, provided he obtains the consent of the chief officer of the district, and engages to bring a certain quantity of salt to the Government store. He is paid at a certain fixed rate of a few pence per maund, and this salt is afterwards sold at a greatly enhanced price. The Government hope by degrees to withdraw from the direct manufacture of salt, and only put a heavy excise duty on the manufactured article.

The salt is made in large pans near the sea-coast during the hottest months of the year. The ground is excavated, puddled and made watertight, and then shallow stretches of sea-water are admitted, which gradually evaporate, leaving the salt deposited on the ground. It is so easy to do this in a small way all along the coast, that a large staff of preventive officers have to be employed to stop the illicit manufacture of salt. The duty is so high, and the process of manufacture so simple, that the poor ryot is constantly tempted to evade the law. The cost of the staff and Government establishment is about one-eighth of the revenue raised. In a poor country like India it is difficult to pay for the cost of government, and this tax, to which the people are accustomed, seems practically to meet the requirements of an universal, yet not burdensome, impost. The manufacture can only be carried on in the dry weather, as one shower of rain would spoil the whole of the salt in the pans.

From Vizagapatam we coasted onwards, touching at Coconada and Masulipatam, but the water was so shallow that we were obliged to anchor three miles from the shore. This prevented us from seeing anything of these towns, and we were glad when on the morning of the 11th January we arrived at Madras.

CHAPTER VIII.

THE Presidency of Madras differs in many respects from the Presidencies of Bengal and Bombay. It has no frontier to guard, no dangerous neighbours to invade it, and no disaffected population to keep in check, and of late years it has had a quiet history. It has thus received scant notice from European politicians, and its affairs are seldom heard of outside its own borders. Its uneventful condition has brought it contempt rather than credit, it has been called "the sleepy Presidency," and civilians in Bengal and Bombay have spoken slightingly of the administration of such a well behaved community. This contemptuous tone is not deserved. Those who know Madras best, find there points of interest which are absent in the other Presidencies. It is no discredit to the administration, but the reverse, that its annals have been uneventful. Wars and rebellions, frontier expeditions and scarcely veiled disloyalty are not matters of congratulation. And though the other Presidencies are oftener mentioned in the English newspapers, yet they do not show better signs of progress or more able administrators.

I found that a soreness existed even amongst the officials, because their affairs were seemingly neglected by the supreme Government, and the feeling that they were unduly put on one side has found expression, I believe, in the Governor's minutes. Certainly the casual traveller finds a number of points of interest in this Presidency, and my stay there was one of the pleasantest parts of my holiday. The temples were more magnificent, the vegetation more tropical, and the English (if possible) kinder than in the other parts of India which I had visited. Above all every parson must be interested in noticing the way in which Christianity has been embraced in this Presidency. The numbers of native Christians are larger than in any other part of India, and here there are whole villages inhabited entirely by Christians under the care of native clergymen. Each of these points roused my interest, and will be hereafter touched upon.

The history of the foundation of Madras may be shortly stated. The first factory was opened there in 1639, under the title of Fort St. George, and for more than a hundred years the growth of this trade depôt was uneventful and continuous. But in the 18th century the French and English contended for the mastery of India, and Madras became the prize of the French in 1746. These were the days of Clive and Dupleix, who wrestled together, each for his distant king, who hardly knew how severe was the struggle, or how far-reaching would be the effects, of this contest waged in the far East. Madras was restored to the English in 1749, by the treaty of Aix-la-Chapelle, and has never since been taken from us. It was in great danger in 1780, when Hyder Ali of Mysore and his son Tipu defeated the English forces, and ravaged the country up to its very walls. But this was only a short-lived triumph for the native arms, and in the later years of the century the ruler of Mysore was driven back, and Madras became the capital of the Presidency which now bears its name.

The city itself is built on a most unpropitious site, on the edge of an unquiet sea, and with a sandy waste behind it. Yet it has increased and flourished in spite of natural disadvantages. It now extends for nine miles along the shore, its population is 400,000, and its trade is very great. The chief disadvantage is the want of a harbour, and many efforts have been made to improve the port. Originally there was only an open roadstead, and passengers and cargo had to be landed in open boats through a surf which was heavy in the calmest weather, and almost impassable in storms. But a large breakwater and pier were built a few years ago, and the harbour was thus for a time made secure. But this improvement did not last long, as Madras was visited by a destructive cyclone, which tore the great coping-stones from their fastenings, and buried them in the sea. The whole breakwater was damaged by the violence of the waves, and though it still gives a partial protection to the harbour, yet the surf beats over it at all points. As we entered the harbour, we could see the ragged condition of this once fine work, and we were astonished at the size and weight of the great stones, which had been dashed from their places by the might of the storm.

As soon as our steamer came to anchor, we were surrounded by crowds of boats full of nearly naked boatmen, who all vociferously clamoured for our patronage, and made rapid descents on our luggage, which we had to guard from being carried off piecemeal. This arrival at Madras has been described by many travellers, but it never fails to interest the new comer. The boatmen look like animated bronze statues, and every muscle of their strong bodies is brought into play, as they keep their boats from colliding with the steamer, and strive to steer them nearest the gangway. Every one seems to be shouting at once, and the whole surface of the water is covered with boats, which press around the steamer, and do their best to cut each other out. As we rowed away from the ship, we looked back and saw the great black hull surrounded by a swarm of little boats, looking like some sea monster surrounded by waterflies.

The first thing in Madras that strikes the new comer is the appearance of the people. The natives here are quite a different race to the inhabitants of Bombay and Bengal, of a much darker colour, and with a more African type of feature. Their clothes are put on less neatly, their turbans are more carelessly tied and often forgotten, their hair is allowed to grow, in a long rough mane behind, while the front of the head is shaved up to the crown. All these points of difference arise from their descent. We are here amongst a Dravidian people, who have never been exterminated or driven away by their Aryan conquerors. They may be called one of the Aboriginal races of India, as although there were earlier races who used stone implements, yet their history is entirely lost. The first accounts that we possess are of the contest between the Aryans and the dark races whom they found in possession of India. The Aryan or Indo-Germanic stock, "from which the Bráhman, the Rájput, and the Englishman alike descend,"* invaded India some 3000 years ago, and found it occupied by different races. These races were gradually driven southward, many were broken into fragments, and only exist as hill-tribes or in the depths of impenetrable forests. But the great Dravidian race of the South was never exterminated, and although subdued by the higher civilization of the Aryan race, which pressed in amongst them, they were never broken into fragments. They have intermarried with their conquerors and have given their languages to 46 millions of people in Southern India. Bishop Caldwell recognizes twelve distinct Dravidian languages, of which Tamil, Telugu, and Kánarese are the chief.

These languages are apparently more difficult than those of Northern India, and English is more generally spoken by the natives in the Madras Presidency than elsewhere. The English is of a curious kind. The chief part of the verb which has been learnt by the natives is the present participle. Other moods and tenses are neglected, which certainly simplifies the language. Coolies, boatmen, gharri-drivers, and servants, all speak an English which is peculiar to Southern

* Hunter's *Indian Empire*, p. 89.

India. Your personal servant is called your "boy," though he may be a grey-headed individual. The message-bearers called "chuprassies" in Bengal, and "puttiwallahs" in Bombay, are here called "peons," a name surviving from the days of the Portugese dominion.

The only other fact that need here be mentioned about the natives is the way in which Christianity has increased amongst them. While the percentage of Christians for the whole of India only represents a half per cent. of the total population, it is 6 per cent. in Tinnevelly and Cochin, and it rises to 20 per cent. in the native states of Travancore. Altogether by the census of 1871 there were about one-and-a-half millions of Christians, of which more than a million were Roman Catholics. These figures have been corrected by the census of 1881. From the report of last year we find that the Christians number 1,862,634, of which the Roman Church claims 963,058.

"The lapse of a few years," continues the writer of the Report, "will, I believe, show a very large accession to the numbers of the various Christian churches. The closest observers are almost unanimous in the opinion that the ground has been already cleared for such a movement, but their views are not so much in accord as to the class from which this accession will be made."

This testimony is the more interesting as coming from a Government official, who would not be unduly biassed in favour of missionaries, or over sanguine about their success. The increase of the Christian population in the province of Madras in the ten years 1871–81 is 165,682, or 30·39 per cent. On this point another extract from the Census Report may be given:—

"Both in actual numbers, and in proportion to the general population, Madras stands clear away in front of all other provinces, and if the southernmost part of the Presidency be taken, we find that in a compact tract containing 7,213,843 souls, 365,544 or 5,067 per 100,000 are Christians. It is in no sectarian spirit that this may be declared wholly a matter for congratulation. There is no enlightened Madras Brahman who does not rejoice equally with the missionaries to see the good work of the latter redeeming the degraded castes of Tinnevelly, and the devil-worshippers of South

Canara from their debased cults to a purer faith and a higher morality."

These figures speak for themselves, but I shall be able to describe what I saw amongst the native Christians of Tinnevelly in a future chapter.

I was but a short time in Madras, and was not able to see all the sights in the city. The public buildings are fine, and built along the sea-shore. They are covered with a beautiful stucco, which has the consistency and polish of marble. There is a fine Cathedral, in which there is a monument to Bishop Heber.

A most interesting School of Art has lately been started, where native artists and mechanics are taught to draw, paint, and design, to work in wood and stone, and to make pottery. The object is to enable native manufactures to compete successfully with English goods, and already certain English goods have been beaten out of the market. Inkstands, gallipots, and cells for telegraph batteries are now bought from these works instead of being imported from England. The pottery we saw was like Doulton ware, and was very artistic. The land of India is so overstocked with labour, that any fresh outlet for the artistic talents or mechanical ingenuity of the native worker must do good. This industrial school is an effort to train native workers, and thus to enable them to earn a living by their own powers. The ruins of magnificent buildings still standing show that once there was a great architectural talent and power amongst the natives of India. This power of designing and constructing large palaces and temples has withered away under the hand of oppression. But now that the native feels himself secure and at peace, it may be possible to educate his artistic faculties, and restore to him this power of architectural invention.

From Madras I went by rail to Bangalore, a journey of over 200 miles. It is a large civil and military station, the head-quarters of the Madras army, and the place where the Chief Commissioner of Mysore resides. It bears much the same relation to Madras that Poona does to Bombay. The climate is cooler, as the town is built on high ground. Next to Madras it is the largest town in the Presidency, and it contains over 142,000 people. The cantonments and bungalows are scattered over a large area, and there are European cavalry, infantry, and artillery lines. There are three Government chaplains and four churches, as the area of the town extends over ten square miles. The public gardens are prettily laid out, and there is a small collection of wild beasts. The Chief Commissioner, who is also the Resident at Mysore, lives in a large house built in the Classical style with a deep portico supported by tall stone pillars, which acts as a verandah and keeps the house cool.

I paid a visit to Mr. Ignatius, the native clergyman, who has charge of the native Christians at Bangalore. It was my first sight of a native clergyman, working as in England with charge of a congregation, and the visit was interesting. I found him in a small house close to the little church, where the native Christians collect for worship. He was dressed in native costume, but he spoke English and was well able to carry on a conversation. He gave me much information about his work, and was very pleasant and seemed hard-working and sincere. His congregation consisted chiefly of servants, clerks, and some Sepoy soldiers. The community numbered about 400, the communicant's list was about 100, and at great festivals he had an average of about 50 communicants. He had begun work as a catechist in the Tinnevelly District, had been ordained in 1865, and had only lately been transferred to this post. He has a day-school open to both Christian and heathen boys and girls, which is helped by the Rajah of Mysore, and he has also a small boarding-school for girls. There is daily service, and a weekly Celebration, and every sign of earnest and devoted work. He gave me his only chair, and was most courteous, and glad to give every information.

I had been half afraid of intruding upon him, but his manner was so cordial and he seemed so pleased with me for coming, that I was glad that I had visited him. He had a small library of English theological works, and his conversation was that of an educated man. There are already two hundred native clergymen in India, so the time seems to have arrived when it is not presumptuous to think of a native Indian Church occupying the land. This is the object to be attained, when in the words of Bishop Cotton "indigenous Stigands and Lanfrancs will take the place of foreign Theodores and Augustines." Certainly my visit to Mr. Ignatius at Bangalore gave me a fresh and pleasant idea of the possibilities of a native pastorate, for nothing could have been more simple and unaffected, more sincere and earnest, than his manner and conversation. Such native ministers will attract converts, and help forward the quiet work of edifying the Church, for they will know the manner of life and modes of thought of their fellow countrymen, and will speak in a tongue "understanded of the people."

Mr. Ignatius invited me to come on Sunday morning to an early Celebration at his Church. He said the service would be in Tamil, but it would be a literal translation of the Communion Office in our Prayer Book, and so I should be able to follow the prayers. I was pleased to have this opportunity of joining with a native Christian congregation in a common act of worship. The Church was a small simple building, white-washed inside, with a well-arranged chancel. The floor of the nave was covered with matting, but only about one-third of the space had seats; the rest of the area was left free for those who preferred to sit on the floor. Natives very seldom use seats of any description, and in their own houses they ordinarily sit on the floor. On this account all Churches for natives have large spaces left free. The Christmas decorations were still up in this little Church at Bangalore; they consisted chiefly of paper wreaths and simple texts. The congregation at this early service was small, consisting of about ten communicants; but this number would not be less than the average in many a village in England, numbering about 500 in population. The Sunday on which I was present was no special festival, and this service was the regular weekly Celebration. The percentage of communicants is usually higher in Tinnevelly than it is in England, but this congregation at Bangalore had been for some years neglected, and had only lately begun to revive.

I was very much struck by the reverent way in which the service was conducted. Mr. Ignatius was all in white, wearing a white cassock under his surplice. And when he entered the sanctuary, he slipped off his shoes, and his bare feet were visible under his cassock. This had a most reverent appearance, and was evidently the natural expression of what he thought due to the sacredness of God's House. All natives put off their shoes when they enter the house of a superior. The native clergy in India have kept up the custom in Church, deeming that the place whereon they stand is holy ground.

From Bangalore I paid a hurried visit to Mysore and Seringapatam. Mysore is a native state containing over 29,000 square miles and with a population of more than five millions of people. Its history is interesting, as its rulers of old often crossed swords with the British. In the latter half of the last century it was governed by Hyder Ali, a Mohammedan usurper, who had imprisoned the rightful Hindu King, and professed to rule in his name. The English fought several battles against Hyder with varying success, and on one occasion the Mysore cavalry ravaged the country up to the walls of Madras. But Hyder died in 1782, and was succeeded by his son Tipú (or Tippoo), with whom peace was concluded. But there was a second Mysore war in 1792, when Tipú was defeated by Lord Cornwallis. And finally in 1799 there was a third Mysore war, when Colonel Wellesley besieged and captured the fortress of Seringapatam. It is this last war which is the best known, as it resulted in the defeat and death of Tipú. He was a cruel ruler. He offended his Hindu subjects both by trying to compel them to become Mohammedans, and also by taking all power from their rightful Rajah. Many tales are still told of his abominable cruelties and evil debaucheries. He was always plotting against the English; the French claimed him as their ally, and "Citoyen Tipú," as they called him, was encouraged by them to harass the English settlements. There is now in the Indian Museum in London the figure of a tiger, standing over the body of an English soldier; it moves by clockwork, and when wound up growls and bites the prostrate figure. This was brought from Seringapatam, and was one of Tipú's favourite playthings.

The final destruction of Tipú's forces took place at Seringapatam. This fortress was considered impregnable, and was called the Tiger's Den. Tipú had given himself the name of the Tiger, and appeared in coloured stripes of black and yellow. Our troops were commanded by General (afterwards Lord) Harris, and Colonel Wellesley (afterwards the Duke of Wellington) served under him. The siege was quickly over. The walls were breached and the fort stormed. Tipú was discovered, buried under piles of dead, and the whole of the territory of Mysore was ours. It was considered politic not to annex the State, so a descendant of the Hindu Rajahs, whom Hyder Ali had deposed, was placed on the throne. He had no children, but was allowed to adopt a child, who is the present Maharajah. During the minority of the present ruler the State was most ably administered by Sir James Gordon, who not only made himself beloved by all the inhabitants, but also obtained a great and beneficial influence over the mind of the young Maharajah. The training and education of this young ruler has been a great success; he has had the inestimable advantage of constant intercourse with a highminded and cultivated English gentleman, and his territory has been handed over to him in perfect order. He was given full power in 1881, and is now independent, but expected to follow the advice of the British Resident at his Court.

My journey to Mysore was by the State Railway, which connects Mysore with Bangalore, a distance of 86 miles. The country was thinly populated, the soil poor, and the rock very near to the surface. Crops of rice, castor oil, grain and sugar cane were being cultivated, and the cocoa-nut palm grew in large groves. I was told that the nuts from each tree were worth about five rupees a year, so a grove of palms is a valuable possession. There have been some gold discoveries in the Mysore territory, but so far as I heard the ore does not pay for working. Some are still sanguine as to the future of these gold fields, but the majority of the workings have not hitherto been successful. I heard that "if you put in a sovereign, you would get back ten shillings," and the general opinion seemed to be that no great fortunes would be made.

I arrived at Mysore about 5 p.m., and had time before sunset to climb part of the way up a hill, which is considered sacred, outside the city. This hill is covered with large boulders of rock, and is crowned by a temple. There is a stone staircase up to the summit, which is about 1000 feet high. I had only time to ascend about 600 feet, to a lower plateau, where there is a colossal bull carved out of one immense boulder. This bull is 20 feet high, and 25 feet in length, and is a very striking object. The view from this point was very extensive over the plain of Mysore, with the city lying at one's feet. The descent of the hill was by no means easy, as the stone steps were worn so smooth by the feet of generations of pilgrims, that my boots slipped on them, and I was nearly precipitated to the bottom. However the barefooted "chuprassie," who accompanied me, made me lean all my weight on him, and thus we arrived safely at the bottom.

Next morning I started before sunrise, and drove seven miles to Seringapatam. The great sights there were the fort and city and tombs of Hyder Ali and Tipú Sahib. The fort is built on an island in the river Cauvery, which here divides into two branches, which re-unite lower down. This island is about three miles long, and one mile broad. The fort, which is situated at the northern extremity of this island, was a very strong place, enclosed by double walls and deep moats. The breach was made in the north-west corner, on the side farthest from Madras, and where the attack was least expected. When it was considered practicable, our soldiers crossed the river, and scaled the wall, doing this with a rush in seven minutes. Tipú was slain inside the northern gateway, and his body was discovered under heaps of dead.

I had the pleasure of being shown over the fort by a native apothecary, who was very intelligent; he was a Christian, and spoke English. He took great interest in the traditional accounts of Tipú, and had collected a number of stories, which are repeated by his countrymen, and may be authentic. One of these attributed the sudden success of the final assault to help given to the English from inside. It is said that Tipú had become hated by his Hindu subjects in consequence of his partiality for Mohammedans. His Prime Minister was a Hindu, whose daughter while bathing was outraged by a Mohammedan soldier. Tipú refused to punish the violator, and in consequence the Prime Minister determined to be revenged. He entered into negotiations with the English, arranged the time for the assault, and at that moment weakened the forces which ought to have defended the breach, and thus enabled us to take the city. All the stories and legends about Tipú exhibit him as a cruel, depraved monarch, without pity or toleration for his Hindu subjects, and careless of their rights.

Inside the fort there are still standing two Hindu temples, and one mosque, but all the palace buildings are in ruins. Outside the fort there is a beautiful little summer palace, where Tipú and his wives used to take their pleasure. This is called the Durria-dowlut, and Colonel Wellesley resided there, when he was in command of the town after the siege. The walls and roofs are decorated with paintings and frescoes, which commemorate a victory gained by Tipú over the English.

About half-a-mile from this palace stands the mausoleum, where Hyder and Tipú are buried. It is a domed structure of handsome design, with a deep verandah supported by massive black marble columns. The doors are of carved marble and teak inlaid with ivory, and the whole building is richly finished. In the interior there are three tombs made of black marble, and covered with silken cloths. Here rest the remains of Hyder Ali, his wife, and Tipú Sahib. The walls are painted in yellow and black in imitation of a tiger's stripes, and the black marble gives a peculiarly rich sepulchral effect to the whole building. All these relics of the past are now kept up by Government in consequence of an eloquent and striking minute written by Lord Dalhousie, the great Governor-General. He found these buildings neglected and falling into decay, and in consequence he impressed on the Government the necessity of providing for their adequate repair, for they were not only memorials of the success of the British arms, and architecturally beautiful, but also associated with the early exploits of one who became the Duke of Wellington.

There is one more building, which is worth a visit, at Seringapatam, and that is the Deserted Bungalow, formerly inhabited by a Colonel Scott. Its history has been well told by the talented author of the "*Lays of Ind.*" Colonel Scott was in the employment of the late Maharajah, and resided in this bungalow with his wife and two daughters. In one day he lost all three through cholera. This sad and sudden affliction unhinged his mind, and he fled from the house, and was never heard of again. Whether he committed suicide or left the country was never known; but the late Maharajah gave orders that everything in the house should be left exactly as it then was. All this happened some 80 years ago, and since then no one has lived in the house, nor have any repairs or alterations been attempted. The whole place is given up to decay. Fragments of carpets are rotting on the floors, pianos rust and fall to pieces in the rooms, shreds of musquito curtains still hang to the bedsteads, chairs and tables are almost crumbled away, and damp, and dust, and cobwebs, cover everything.

"The garden about it is tangled and wild,
Sad trees sigh close to its eaves,
And the dark lithe shapes
Of chattering apes
Swing in and out of the leaves;
And when night's dank vapours rise grey and foul,
The silence is rent by the shrill screech-owl.

"The windows are shuttered, the doors are shut,
And the odour and stain of decay
Is on plaster and beam,
And the stone steps seem
To be ooze-corroding away;
And the air all round is as tinged with the breath
Of the felt, though invisible, presence of Death.

"The mouldering rooms are now as they stood
Near eighty years ago:
The piano is there,
And table and chair,
And the carpet rotting slow,
And the beds whereon the corpses lay,
And the curtains half time-mawed away."

I never saw a more desolate-looking, deserted, melancholy spot. The rain has penetrated through the roof, parts of the walls are giving way, the ceilings are falling, and in a few more years there will be only a heap of ruins left to mark the site of this once-pleasant abode on the banks of the Cauvery.

"A type of gloom and decay and death,
And happiness overcast,
Is this bungalow lonely
And tenanted only
By memories of the past.
Peace to the shades of the three who died
In that lonely house by the Cauvery's tide!"

From Seringapatam I took the train back to Bangalore, and on this journey I had a curious experience of the rigid way in which the law of "caste" rules the Hindu population of India. I was travelling in a second-class carriage, and in the next compartment there were three natives, only separated from me by a low partition. One of them was a boy suffering from fever, and parched with thirst. They were all high-caste Brahmins from Gujerat, and were on a pilgrimage to the holy places in the South of India. One of the men with this sick lad was an intelligent, courteous person, speaking good English. I could not help being attracted by the moans of the poor lad, and I heard him asking for water. I knew it would be useless to offer my water-bottle to them, as they would not drink from any vessel which I had used. Still as it was a case of emergency, I ventured to make the offer as politely as I could. I was not surprised at its being courteously refused; but the younger of the two men asked me to call the station master at the next station, and get him to obtain a drink of water for them. He thought as I was an Englishman, my request would be more likely to be attended to. When the train stopped, I called the station master and told him what they wanted. But as soon as he saw them, he shook his head. He explained that he he had no "bhîsti" (water-carrier) at that station of high enough caste to give these gentlemen water. They were superior to ordinary people, and though the bhîsti at most stations is chosen from a high caste, in order that he may be able to minister to everyone's wants, yet my fellow-travellers were of a higher caste than the bhîsti at that station, and therefore could not have their drinking vessels filled by him without suffering contamination. So we were no further forward, and the poor sick lad had to go on enduring his raging thirst without alleviation. Yet there was no hint on his part of a wish to break through the rules of his religion, and he seemed ready to endure any suffering rather than do what he felt to be wrong. It was an example of consistency and rectitude, which many a Christian might imitate with advantage. However, at the next station his sufferings were relieved. As soon as we stopped, one of the men got out with his drinking vessel, and soon came back radiant with joy. He explained that he had found a well from which he had drawn the water himself, and as no one else had touched it, this water was lawful for them to drink. So the sick lad got his sufferings relieved, and I learnt a lesson of the heaviness of the yoke which "caste" puts on the necks of the Hindu population.

From Bangalore I travelled southwards, *viâ* Erode and Trichinopoly, to Tanjore. The great sights of the South of India are the enormous temples, which are peculiar to this district. These temples are covered with carving, they often cover several acres of ground, and they are as much superior in size and richness to those in the North of India, as the Cathedrals of England are to the Parish Churches.

Hinduism in this part of India is a living religion. There are but few Mohammedans, and nearly all the natives are Hindus. The majority of them belong to the sect which worships Vishnu as the chief god, and their foreheads are slashed with a sort of trident mark, viz.: two perpendicular white lines which are drawn from the roots of the hair to the eyebrows, where they meet in a curve, while between them there is a red mark in the centre of the forehead. This mark is very noticeable, and gives a sinister expression to the face. It represents, I believe, the two footprints of Vishnu, which remind his votaries of his incarnations. These incarnations of Vishnu are the most popular gods of modern Hinduism. He is worshipped as Krishna all through Southern India, and the story of his adventures, when he took on himself this form, are amongst the best known of all the sacred legends. This desire for a visible, and so to speak human god is universal amongst the mass of the people, who cannot understand difficult doctrines or abstruse philosophy. The Brahmans have invented various legends, which represent Vishnu as taking on himself different shapes for the purpose of preserving the world when in danger. These legends describe his adventures and various doings. His actions were by no means always seemly, neither can his conduct be always justified. The result is that the mass of the people worship a god, whose life is full of astounding and foolish incidents, and whose actions were sometimes immoral and indecent. No wonder that such a religion has failed to purify its adherents, and that the temples of the god are often centres of immorality and sinks of iniquity. The longing for a visible God and a true Incarnation seems to be an instinct in human nature.

At Tanjore I first saw one of those enormous temples for which Southern India is famous. It stands in the middle of the city, and its great central mass is seen from afar towering upwards to the height of 200 feet. It may be taken as an example of all the temples of Southern India, and a description of its arrangements will serve to explain the design of all these remarkable structures. Fergusson * says that these temples consist almost invariably of the four following parts. The *vimana* or shrine, containing a cell in which the image of the god or his emblem is placed. This is always square in plan, and surmounted by a pyramidal roof of one or more stories. Then the *mantapas* or porches, which always cover or

* *Handbook of Architecture*, vol. i., p. 88.

precede the door leading to the cell. Thirdly the gate pyramids, or *gopuras*, leading into the quadrangular enclosure which surrounds the *vimana*. And lastly the *choultries*, or pillared halls, which are used for various purposes. Besides these a temple always contains tanks or wells of water, to be used either for sacred purposes or for the convenience of the priests, dwellings for the various grades of the priesthood, and numerous other buildings.

This temple at Tanjore Fergusson calls "the most splendid temple in India." Entering through a gateway surmounted by a *gopura* or lofty gate pyramid, one finds oneself in a large quadrangle paved with stone. Each side of this quadrangle is 200 yards long, and all round there runs a colonnade which forms a cloister. In the centre of the great court rises the *vimana*, the shrine itself, which is stupendous in size and covered with the richest carvings. Each side of the base of this building measures 82 feet, and it is two stories high; but upon this structure there rises a pyramidal roof of 14 stories, finishing in a dome-shaped apex, surmounted with a gilt spike. The whole height is 200 feet, and each of the four sides of this lofty structure is covered with carving. There are numerous niches in which figures are placed, and the light and shade are very marked and have a striking effect. The building was erected about 800 years ago, and has been probably repaired at some later date. The porch, or *mantapa*, in this temple is subordinate to the central shrine, and the whole design is more clearly visible than in some other temples. In the great court-yard facing the principal entrance of the shrine there is a colossal bull carved out of one mass of rock, and saturated with oil. It rests upon a platform raised on 12 steps, and is covered with a lofty canopy. In the colonnade round the inside wall of the quadrangle there are various frescoes portraying the incarnations of Vishnu and exploits of heroes; there are also several idolatrous symbols, and indecent paintings. But though all the details will not bear inspection, yet the great size of the central court-yard, the way in which the shrine stands out, and the richness of the carving render this temple quite unique.

After I had visited the temple I went to a small church in which there was a monument to the Danish missionary, Schwartz, erected in 1798 by the then Maharajah of Tanjore. Schwartz had a wonderful influence over natives, and was much respected by them. He acted as ambassador between Clive and the native princes, and one Rajah on his death-bed appointed the missionary to act as guardian to his infant son. He was revered by all the people of Tanjore, many of whom were converted to Christianity by his means, and when he died in 1798 all classes of the people mourned for him. There is a mission in Tanjore now carried on by the Society for the Propagation of the Gospel, but I had no opportunity of seeing any of the workers in it. The church in which Schwartz's monument is placed is in a disgracefully dirty condition, and is now very seldom, if ever, used for service. The Rajah of Tanjore, who was such an admirer of Schwartz, and who was nearly converted to Christianity, has been succeeded by less respectable rulers, and the present condition of the kingdom is not satisfactory. There is no Rajah at present, the Ranee is pensioned, and an English civilian receives the revenues of the state.

I visited the Palace, and was shown some of the outer courts and rooms. It was like other princely residences in India, very dirty, very tawdry, and overflowing with idle retainers greedy for rupees. The building covered a very large area, and within its *enceinte* there were numerous court-yards and passages, barracks and stabling, servant's residences and rooms for crowds of dependents. In one court-yard the royal elephants were picketed, and their trappings, used on great occasions of state, were very magnificent. But mixed up with these really beautiful specimens of native workmanship I was also shown common coloured pictures of the cheapest kind, and beautiful native garments of cloth of gold were kept in cases, which were flanked by vulgar English ornaments and coloured prints. I believe the library holds a really valuable collection of Sanscrit MSS., but these were not shown. The books that I saw were neither beautiful nor curious.

How best to treat the princely families of India is a constantly recurring difficulty. If the ruling member of the house is inclined to be amenable to Western influences, he may become partially Anglicized, and then he takes his position as a great landowner, and the management of his estate may afford him sufficient occupation. But if he lives in the same way as did his forefathers, he finds himself in a difficult position. He is a ruler without power, trammelled by law, and prevented from doing what his ancestors did. He sees no career open to him. He will not take to the army as a profession, for he could not brook to be controlled by English officers, and he cannot govern his principality in his own way for all independent power has been taken from him. Many native princes pass an idle, objectless life. They spend their days in smoking, and eating, and dissipation at home, or in paying visits to each other with all the pomp they can command; they multiply useless retainers, which they think add to their grandeur, and they often waste their resources by extravagance and excess. They have been likened to the Barons of the Middle Ages, but their lot is harder, for they have no voice in the government of their country, nor any career open to them. It is hoped that the younger generation may become better educated, and as local government spreads, they may be able to take a share in ordering the affairs of their neighbourhood. But their position is a difficult one, and their future lot is one of the problems which the rulers of India will have to face.

CHAPTER IX.

FROM Tanjore I travelled to Trichinopoly, where I first saw some of the Mission work of Southern India. Trichinopoly is a large city, containing a population of 76,000 people, and famous for its silver carving and paintings on talc. The most striking feature is the great Rock, which towers up, like a lesser Gibraltar, in the midst of the town. This rock is a great block of gneiss, which rises up to a height of 400 feet. It is quite bare of vegetation, its sides are very steep, and its mass rises up abruptly from the plain. The view of it from a distance is very fine, and this bold rock is seen long before the town is reached. The top of it is crowned with a temple, which is reached by a steep stone staircase covered by a richly carved colonnade. Above the great temple there is a further ascent to the extreme apex of the rock, and this has to be made on the smooth surface of the stone without either covering or balustrade. The steep slope of the stone and its slippery condition render this an awkward climb, but the view from the top repays one for the difficulty of the ascent. Beneath one's feet the city lies, laid out like a map, with broad, straight streets and houses embowered in palms. Round the north side of the rock flows the river Cauvery, a broad and swift stream with banks covered with cocoa-nuts and its islands green with feathery trees. About three miles distant are seen the gate pyramids and pinnacles of the great temple of Srirangham, and far away on all sides extends the great plain covered with paddy, and looking most rich and fertile. The whole of this district is irrigated with water taken from the Cauvery, and the system of trenches and tanks utilizes every drop of the life-giving streams.

Besides the rock of Trichinopoly the great temple of Srirangham is well worth a visit. A drive of about three miles brought us to the island on which this wonderful mass of buildings has been erected. Originally there was probably a small shrine over some sacred relic, or idol. But this *sanctum sanctorum* has been surrounded by successive enclosures with lofty gate pyramids, till the central shrine has been dwarfed and concealed by the magnificent and lofty structures within which it has been enclosed. The plan of the building is square, and the central temple is surrounded by seven square court-yards, one within the other. Each of these encircling walls is pierced by four great gateways, one on each side. Thus from whichever side you approach this holy temple you must pass through seven great gateways, until you came to the central shrine. The gate pyramids are very lofty, and covered with carved figures. The outermost are the tallest, and they gradually decrease in size as the innermost shrine is approached. Thus "the inner enclosure being 200 or 300 feet square, the gate pyramid is only 40 or 50 feet broad, and the passage through it 10 or 12 feet wide, and 18 or 20 feet high, while the outer ones, standing in walls 2475 and 2880 feet in extent, are 130 feet wide by 100 feet deep, the opening 21 feet 6 inches wide by twice that in height."* This gives the proportions only of the openings in the *gopuras*, but the height of the whole gopura must be more than 100 feet high, and Fergusson calls these gateways "the most stupendous buildings of the South of India." The whole of the temple buildings cover half a square mile of ground, and the outer circuit of the walls is more than two miles in circumference. The best view of this mass of buildings is obtained by ascending to the top of one of the gate pyramids. From this point the circuit of the walls can be traced, the diminishing squares of

* Fergusson, vol. i., p. 92.

the court-yards are plainly visible, and the towering masses of the numerous *gopuras* show where the lines of entrance pierce the enclosing walls. As the eye traces these successive diminishing squares, it at last rests on the gilt spike which surmounts the roof of the innermost shrine. This is often the lowest point in the structure, and thus the lowliest thing of all is the *sanctum sanctorum* of the temple. The same thing is true of the internal arrangements. You pass through magnificent gateways, the jambs of which are formed of single blocks of granite at least 40 feet in length. You cross broad streets full of life and colour, trodden by countless worshippers and gay with stalls where fruit and flowers and various offerings are sold. You pass by wide tanks with stone steps leading down to clear water, and surrounded by colonnades formed of carved pillars. You thread great halls supported by thousands of stone columns, which are carved with all the grotesque richness so typical of Hindu art. And finally you penetrate into a dark and malodorous hall, where the priests check your further advance. And from within there comes a sound of gabbled prayers and high-pitched nasal chanting, with the smell of incense and the ring of bells; and as you try to pierce the darkness of the dimly lighted shrine, part of a misshapen figure, or a blotch of vermilion colour, is all that is visible. Before this thousands of worshippers are prostrating themselves at full length in the dust. Here candles are lighted, offerings are made, and the whole worship of the temple service culminates. For this all the lofty gate pyramids and pillared halls have been erected, and the magnificence of the outside architecture is but a screen to the meanness and dirt and darkness of the central shrine. It may truly be said to be typical of the religion. For the more you penetrate into its recesses, the less beauty you find in it. The closer you touch idolatry, the more loathsome it appears. The very shrine is a cloak for immorality, the ritual encourages vice, and the worshippers love darkness rather than light because their deeds are evil.

It was interesting to turn from these scenes where idolatry was rampant, and learn how a few earnest missionaries were trying to lead these crowds of heathen to a purer faith and a higher life. The work of the Society for the Propagation of the Gospel Mission at Trichinopoly has had many difficulties to contend with, but it is now moving forward in a promising way. The number of Christian clergy and teachers is miserably inadequate to the work. The whole district extends over 2116 square miles, about the size of the county of Norfolk, and the population is about 800,000. In this large area there are one English and three native clergymen working, besides a few catechists and school teachers. There are altogether 17 Christian congregations, numbering 1434 souls. The communicants number 697, nearly one-half of the entire number of Christians. These statistics are taken from a Report given to me by the Rev. J. L. Wyatt, missionary in charge. He himself lives in the town of Trichinopoly, and exercises a general oversight over the whole district. In those villages where he cannot be present himself, it is the duty of the catechists to conduct services, to instruct (so far as they can) the members of the different congregations, to visit the sick, and to make known the Gospel. This work of the catechist is most useful. He is always a native, and speaks to the people in familiar words and in their own language. He keeps the congregation together, and acts under the superintendence of the English missionary. It is impossible for the English clergyman to visit these outlying villages very often, as his time is fully occupied by arduous and important work in the large towns. But his hands are strengthened and his work prevented from languishing by the humble and quiet labours of the resident native catechists. These native Christian teachers chiefly come from the district of Tinnevelly, where the training of such humble preachers of the

Gospel has formed a large and useful part of the Christian work done in that part of India. Other portions of the country are now being benefited by their efforts, and a great part of the quiet Christian life in the smaller villages is due to the unobtrusive work of the native catechist.

The mission work at Trichinopoly, as elsewhere, is largely done through its schools. These schools are of various sizes and of different classes, and range from the most elementary village school up to a high school which prepares its scholars for matriculation at the University of Madras. A few words on these schools will show how large a part of the missionary's time and thoughts is taken up with education, and how useful an instrument it is in the evangelization of the people of India.

The chief feature of this mission is the great High School under the Society for the Propagation of the Gospel in the town of Trichinopoly. It is a grand institution, the largest school outside the Presidency town of Madras. It had (in 1880) 196 boys on the register. The Principal is a layman, and there are 27 native assistants with him, about one-half of whom are non-Christians. Scriptural instruction is given for one hour daily by the Christian teachers to all the classes. I was unfortunately unable to see this great school at work, as it was holiday time when I was at Trichinopoly. But from all I could hear the school is doing good work, it is attended by crowds of heathen boys who desire to receive a good education and to matriculate at the University, and it is deservedly popular. All over India the desire for an English education is very great, for the knowledge of English opens the way to Government employ; thus the brightest and most intelligent of the heathen lads flock to the classes and crowd the rooms of the S.P.G. College. They thus come under the influence of Western thought and civilization, and their own superstitions are broken down. Even if for a time the educated natives profess to be Materialists, and seem to have lost their former faith without obtaining anything in its place, there is no need to despair; for there is no vitality and no beauty in modern Hinduism, and we may trust that the native, whose old idolatry has been shattered by modern education, although he may pass through a dark phase of doubt and atheism, will not be the loser. It is a gain to have overthrown idolatry, and when the ruins are swept away, something purer, and truer, and more lasting will often be erected in its place.

The missionary exerts but little direct influence through the classes at the High School. Any evangelistic results that can be traced to the teaching there given, spring from the effect produced indirectly by the life and conversation of the Christian teacher on his pupils. But there are in Trichinopoly other schools, which are markedly of a missionary character. There is a large boys' boarding school, a girls' boarding school, a female training institution, and nine girls' and seven boys' day schools. In these various schools there are altogether 489 boys and 449 girls, so nearly 1000 children are under Christian instruction.

I visited the boys' boarding school, which now gives accommodation to about 50 boarders. This is located in an old District Sessions Court, which, being no longer required by the Government, was offered for sale. Mr. Wyatt advised the Madras Committee of the Society for the Propagation of the Gospel to buy the house, and they did so for a very moderate sum. The buildings are large and commodious, and stand in a good compound of five acres of ground. The school will accommodate about 200 boys, and one large room 40 feet by 24 feet is used as a chapel. Those of the boarders who can afford it, pay something towards their maintenance, and thus they learn to be independent. But the great aim of the institution is, in Mr. Wyatt's words, to "secure boys for the school, of good families, irrespective of the fees they are able to pay, so that *they* may obtain a good religious education and thereby recommend the Christian religion to the people of their respective villages, and that *we* may obtain material for our future native agents. Christian boys of the rural villages have no opportunity of receiving a religious education in their homes, and some that have been taken into the school are, as regards religious knowledge, hardly removed a step from the heathen boys round them; in fact, they do not know anything like the amount of Scripture that heathen boys know who live in the town and attend Mission Schools." This system of keeping boarding schools under the care of the English missionary has been found to answer very well in Tinnevelly, and it seems likely to have a good effect everywhere, as the personal intercourse between the scholars and the English clergyman is sure to act beneficially. From this intercourse conversions are likely to spring, and the Christian boys in the school influence their heathen companions. Indeed many of the heathen boys are desirous of being baptized, but while they are young they are not admitted to Baptism without their parents' consent. There was an interesting case in 1882, when one of these lads was baptized. His father was a heathen, but had in his boyhood attended a mission school. He was induced by some Christian friends to place his son in the boarding school, and occasionally he came to see him. This gave the missionary an opportunity of talking to him about the Christian religion, and the father said he had never forgotten the lessons he had learned at school when young, but as his wife and many of his friends were opposed to Christianity he remained in heathenism. However, his son soon expressed a wish to be baptized, and persuaded his father to be baptized also. This he consented to do, and both son and father were baptized together. The wife still remains in heathenism, but has ceased to express any opposition to Christianity, and there is a hope that she will soon follow the example of her husband and son. This is an instance of the influence exercised over the scholars in the boarding school, and it shows what a distinctly evangelistic agency a good school may be.

Besides the boys' boarding school there is also a girls' boarding school containing 52 children, and a female training institution for teachers. The latter is a most useful institution, as it supplies teachers for the different day schools in the town and in the various villages. There are besides 24 day schools, for both boys and girls, under the supervision of the missionary, where some 800 children, both Christian and heathen, are under instruction. Some of these are in the outlying villages and some in the town of Trichinopoly. There ought of course to be many more, and if every village and large town in the district were properly occupied, the schools would be counted by hundreds. There is no better way of influencing for good the rising generation than by efficient Christian schools, and I think those missionaries are very wise, who throw much of their strength into educational work.

The boarding schools and day schools occupy much of Mr. Wyatt's time, but he does not neglect the more direct evangelistic work, by which he tries to influence the heathen who are dwelling around him. One of the most interesting ways in which this work is attempted is an evening meeting which is held in a school-room twice a week for non-Christians. These meetings are very well attended, and seem to be popular. Mr. Wyatt says that the same faces appear week by week, and the numbers vary from 180 to 300. The mode of procedure is to start with a procession of a few boys, who go singing through the streets to the place of meeting. The Tamils of Southern India are very musical, and there are a number of native tunes which are very popular; to some of these suitable words have been placed, and they are thus made into Christian lyrics. The singing procession soon collects a crowd, and the school is filled with an attentive audience.

Once the procession was interrupted by a little stone-throwing, and once a snake was introduced into the meeting to create an excitement, but the proceedings generally pass off quietly. When the lyric or hymn is finished, there is a short prayer, a portion of Scripture is read, and then there is an address given on some religious topic, such as God, Man, Sin, Worship, Prayer, Christ, or the like. Then anyone is invited to speak, or to ask questions, and after a discussion the meeting closes with more hymns. The proceedings are all in Tamil, and the address is generally given by one of the native clergymen, who are working with Mr. Wyatt.

I was fortunate enough to be at Trichinopoly on one of the evenings when these meetings are held, and I was thus an eye-witness of the scene. We got to the place after the audience had assembled, and during the delivery of the address. The room was close to the street, and open on all sides to the road, being little more than a large shed supported on wooden pillars, and with a few benches in the centre. It was dimly lighted with a few oil lamps, and was fairly filled with about a hundred people, who came and went as they pleased. At the upper end of the room there was a table, behind which stood a little knot of native Christians, some teachers and choir boys, and the native clergyman. The rest of the room was filled with a heathen crowd, the more regular attendants sat on the benches in the centre, others stood round the pillars half in and half out of the room; some seemed to have been attracted by curiosity and stayed but a short time, but the majority remained throughout the proceedings. The address, which was delivered by the native clergyman, was of course unintelligible to me, but I was told afterwards that he was comparing Christ with other religious teachers, and showing how far superior were the doctrines He taught to those promulgated by Hindu teachers. The address was extremely fluent, and I was told that its matter was likewise excellent. Certainly he gained the attention of all, and the people listened silently during the whole of the address. Though I could understand no word of what was said, yet I could not help being interested. The bare room open on all sides, the two or three lamps lighting up the speaker, the keen dark faces with heathen signs painted on their foreheads peering out round every pillar, the seats in the centre filled with men who listened with rapt attention, the stream of foreign speech pouring forth in fluent gutturals, the eloquent action of the native preacher who seemed full of his subject, all made a picture which lives in my memory. When the address was over, discussion was invited, and an objection was promptly raised by someone in the room. I was told afterwards what was said. The objector found fault with the preacher for having said that the Hindus worshipped devils, and he said this description of Hinduism was not fair or just. He was patiently heard, and was not allowed to be interrupted, though some of the Christian catechists were anxious to do battle with him before he had finished. When he had done, Mr. Wyatt quoted two instances of devil worship which had come under his own observation, and the audience seemed convinced of the justness of the phrase objected to. There is a great deal of low fetishism, underlying popular Hinduism, prevalent in the country districts, and though the educated men of the town may not approve of it, yet this degraded religion of fear, and this notion of propitiating invisible beings who would do harm if not appeased, is common amongst the unlearned. The audience seemed ready to applaud the points made on either side, and I was much struck with the patience and good sense of the reply. There was no wish to gain a mere dialectic advantage, or to hurt the feelings of an opponent, but the main desire was to win the objector to the side of the truth, and to show him that there had been a justification for the obnoxious phrase. We left the room after this before the proceedings had quite terminated, but I had seen enough to understand something of the difficulty and yet the hopefulness of evangelistic work.

From Trichinopoly I went by train to Madura, where there is another of the great temples of Southern India. The area covered by the buildings is hardly so great as that of the great temple at Srirangham, but the carving is much richer. The temple at Madura also stands in the centre of the town, and is therefore fuller of life, and constantly thronged with crowds of people. The great gate pyramids are covered with sculptured figures, and the whole of the front of the *gopura* is picked out in red, and blue, and green, and gold. The plan of the temple is similar to that at Srirangham, consisting of a small central shrine enclosed by rectangular encircling walls. Between the successive squares of these walls there are broad streets, and in these and in the principal approaches there are bazaars, where every kind of article is exhibited for sale. Brass and metal work of all sorts, fruit and flowers, china and glass from England, cloths and silks; the courts are full of a bargaining, gossiping, chaffering crowd who turn the whole temple into a place of merchandise. At intervals the crowd is thrust aside by the advent of one of the trustees of the temple, or a great Rajah goes by with pomp and retinue. Or one of the great temple elephants comes slowly swinging along, bearing water for the shrine, his trunk daubed with vermilion and his head wreathed with flowers. I believe this temple possesses great store of jewels and precious stones, which are said to be of incalculable value, but I was not fortunate enough to get a sight of the treasure. But the chief thing which render this temple noticeable amongst all its compeers is the richness of the stone carving of the pillars. Hindu art is here at its best, and the figure sculpture is truer to nature than anywhere else. The pillars are carved in very high relief, and are covered with numerous male and female figures placed in attitudes of rapid action.

The most striking part of this great temple is the *choultry* or pillared hall, built by Trimul Naik in 1623. These *choultries* are common in all temples, and are of various sizes. They are used as halls of ceremony, as places where the car of the god is kept, and as covered colonnades where the dancing girls attached to the temple dance and sing. The one at Madura was built by the King to provide a suitable abode for the god, who is said to have consented to leave his temple for ten days every year and visit the King, if a fit building was provided for his reception. The *choultry* is certainly a wonderful structure, consisting of a great hall 333 feet long and 81 feet wide, supported by 123 pillars. These pillars are the great feature of the building, as they are all covered with the most elaborate ornamentation. No two of them are alike, they stand about nine feet apart, and the appearance of the hall is that of a forest of stone piers, the diversity and richness of which bewilder the eye. The cost of this great hall is said to have been a million sterling, and it took 22 years to complete. When it is remembered that this pillared hall is only a part of the whole design of the temple, and that there are numerous other corridors and cloisters, gate-pyramids and porches, all covered from top to bottom with carvings of all kinds, the amount of labour that has been expended on this great temple is inconceivable. Most of the stone seemed to be a close-grained granite, and the whole has been done by native artists without any help from European designers. The failure in the design is the want of a good *coup d'œil*, but the labour of construction and the care bestowed on the stone sculpture are amazing.

Close alongside the temple are the remains of the Palace of Trimul Naik, which is now being restored by Government. Its great feature is the large Hall of Audience supported by more than 125 columns, which seemed to be about the size of Westminster Hall. The centre of this hall is very spacious and lofty, and the columns are arranged in a double and treble cloister, the roof of which must be 50 feet high. When the Prince of Wales visited Madura, he was received in this great hall, and an elephant stood before each pillar. So that the Prince passed up through a double row of these great creatures to the throne set for him at the end of the hall. Besides this great hall there are other smaller halls attached, which are all richly carved, and now used as public offices and judicial courts. Trimul Naik was a contemporary of the great Moguls, who erected the magnificent buildings at Delhi and Agra. He must have been equally powerful in Southern India, and capable of commanding any amount of labour.

Another striking sight at Madura is a great tank, about 200 yards square, in which there is a small island on which a carved temple stands. This is an object of pilgrimage at certain seasons, when the waters of the tank are covered with a numerous flotilla of boats.

Mission work at Madura is chiefly in the hands of an American society, whose schools are highly spoken of, and whose labours are reported to be successful.

The English Churchmen have built a beautiful little church for their own use, and a chaplain is provided by a Madras society for providing additional clergy in India. The status of the English Church in India is one which is open to criticism. At present chaplains are provided at the large stations by Government, and are paid out of Government funds. They are considered to be primarily for the use of the troops, but there are some chaplains which are appointed to civil stations. The question has been raised whether it is justifiable to tax the natives of India to support an ecclesiastical establishment for the use of our soldiers and officials. The cost of this establishment is over £200,000 a year. The argument in favour of the retention of this charge on the revenues of the country is that it is as much part of our system of administration in India as charges for doctors or pensions. The civilians expect to have religious privileges provided for them, just as they expect to have free doctoring and large retiring allowances. It is part of the bargain made with them, when they take service under the Indian Government, and it is one of their privileges which they take into consideration, when they determine to expatriate themselves to India.

But now the Government is withdrawing chaplains from nearly all civil stations where there are no troops, and the civilians are expected to combine and provide the salary of a clergyman, if they desire his services. Also the planters in many of the tea and coffee districts pay for their own clergyman. And in every diocese in India there is now a society for the employment of additional clergy, which is supported by voluntary subscriptions, and which provides funds for the salary of a clergyman in places where there are sufficient Europeans to render one necessary. At Madura the resident civilians have built a beautiful Church, and have secured the services of a clergyman. If all civil stations were to act in like manner, English Churchmen would not have to appeal to the Government to provide them with their religious privileges. The chaplains might then be retained only for the use of the troops, and the Church would be benefited by thus being forced to depend more on voluntary effort. The services of the clergyman would be more appreciated when the congregation had learnt that it was their duty to support him, and that "the labourer was worthy of his hire."

From Madura I travelled southwards into the district of Tinnevelly. This is the name most often heard at Missionary meetings at home, and when the Christian Missions of India are referred to, it is this district which is generally mentioned. For here may be seen whole villages entirely Christian, built round the Church, and the villagers themselves support a resident clergyman, who is often a native. It is the one part of

India where Christianity is the religion of a distinct proportion (6 per cent.) of the population. Instead of being professed by a few converts, it is here the faith of thousands, who have been brought up from childhood within its borders. I had seen many missionaries in various parts of India struggling with the overwhelming masses of heathendom. I was now to see that district where even the most sceptical as to the good done by missionaries must confess that a modicum of success has crowned their labours. After having seen the efforts made to evangelize the heathen, it was pleasant to anticipate the sight of Christian villages where temples and idols were unknown.

The district of Tinnevelly extends from a little south of Madura to Cape Comorin. It is bounded on the east and south by the coastline of India, and on the west by the native States of Travancore and Cochin. The soil is sandy and poor, and the chief wealth of the district comes from the Palmyra palms, which are very numerous. It is a district away from railways. The line from Madras has its terminus at the town of Tinnevelly, but those who desire to penetrate further into the country must be content with the slow progress and jolting motion of the "bandy" or bullock waggon. The people are quiet and inoffensive, originally very ignorant, and prone to devil-worship. They were the aboriginal inhabitants of the land, and had never heartily embraced Hinduism, but preferred to combine with it many of their old superstitions.

More than a hundred years ago the district was visited by Schwartz, but it was not till fifty years later that any great effort was made to evangelize this people. From the very first the idea of the missionaries was to found villages entirely Christian, where the tumults and seductions of heathenism should be unknown. This idea has never been lost sight of, and now it has been realized in numerous instances. In 1841 Mr. Caldwell (now Bishop Caldwell) began his great work, and his name will always be associated with the Tinnevelly Mission. He not only succeeded in adding greatly to the number of Churches, and schools, and clergymen, and catechists in the district, but he started a scheme of local Church government and self-sustentation which has answered admirably. There is a Church council in every district, which the clegyman consults in all matters of local interest, and which assists him in collecting and distributing the offerings made by the congregation. So well has the Church been organized, that nearly every congregation supports its native pastor, and also subscribes largely to spread the Gospel news to the neighbouring heathen villages. These poor Christians of Tinnevelly set an example worth noting by richer congregations in England.

The rise of the native pastorate is one of the most interesting facts in connection with the Tinnevelly Mission. In 1841 there were in the whole district seven European clergy and only one native. In 1869 there were fourteen European and forty-seven native clergymen. This number has since then been largely increased. In 1877 a fresh departure was made. The Tinnevelly Missions were put under the joint charge of Dr. Caldwell and Dr. Sargent, who were together consecrated Assistant-Bishops to the Bishop of Madras. Bishop Caldwell was to have charge of the Missions under the Society for the Propagation of the Gospel, while Bishop Sargent was to exercise oversight over the Church Missionary Society's Missions. Thus the district of Tinnevelly has two Bishops resident within its borders, both of whom know the native languages, and are able to foster the growth of the native Church.

The same year was marked by the terrible famine which devastated all Southern India, and was grievously felt in Tinnevelly. The failure of the rain caused loss of crops; bullocks died and wells dried up; the people looked out on bare fields and no food; the heavens were brass, and the earth iron; and multitudes died before relief could be brought to their doors. Numbers of half-starved, emaciated people, men, and women, and children, crawled to the relief camps, where grain was distributed. Numbers more were found in a dying state by the roadside, and were carried to places where food could be obtained. All England was stirred by the news which was sent home. Large sums were given for the relief of distress, and thousands of lives were saved by the labours of an army of almoners. The after-result in Tinnevelly was most striking. When the heathen saw this flood of charity poured out on them from strangers in a far distant land, they could not but feel grateful to their unknown benefactors. Then followed a desire to know more about this religion, which inculcated such beneficent charity. So there was a movement and a stirring all through the land, and in 1878 there was a marked desire to hear more about Christianity. Numbers of villages placed themselves under Christian instruction, and the accessions from heathenism were so marked, that it was rightly called a "harvest of souls." The numbers of those under instruction suddenly increased from 23,000 to 43,000. And "the principal cause of the movement was undoubtedly the conviction that generally prevailed, that whilst Hinduism had left the famine-stricken to die, Christianity had stepped in like an angel from heaven, to render them in their distress the sincerest sympathy and the most effectual succour." So Bishop Caldwell writes, and he also notices that in no case was an agreement to become Christians made a condition for the receiving of relief. Indeed the great accession of converts took place after the season of famine was over, and when all relief had stopped. The distribution of money and grain during the distress was made without any conditions, and in every place men could obtain relief without changing their religion. Every witness seems to agree that the movement towards Christianity was quite spontaneous and arose simply from the fact that the hearts of the people had been touched and softened by the extraordinary kindness shown to them in their distress by the Christians of England.

Since 1878 the tide of accessions to Christianity has continued to flow, and the increase has been regular and unceasing. Probably now the total number of Christians in Tinnevelly under the care of the various societies in connection with the Church of England does not fall short of 100,000. There is of course an immensity more to be done. Missionaries returning home and wishing to interest apathetic audiences are inclined to magnify their success and dwell much on the immense strides which have been made in the last few years. All this is perfectly true, and worthy to be remembered. The increase of the Christian population in the province of Madras in the ten years 1871–81 is 165,682, or 30·39 per cent. This is a fact which should make us thankful and hopeful. But we also need to remember how small is the number of Christians when contrasted with the multitude of heathen amongst whom they live. The total numbers for the whole of India are, Hindus about 188 millions, and Mohammedans 50 millions. The number of Christians is only 1,853,426, not much more than a half per cent. of the total population of India. Even in Tinnevelly, where Christians apparently abound in far greater numbers than elsewhere, where there are native Christian villages, and native clergy, and numerous native Churches, even there the Christians number barely 6 per cent. of the population. Thus out of every hundred people in Tinnevelly there are still 94 who worship idols, or profess some false religion. The numbers in India are so enormous that it is difficult to realize what multitudes of people there are who have never heard a sound of the Gospel message.

CHAPTER X.

MY journey from Madura to Tinnevelly was hot, and tiring, and dusty. I started at 5 a.m., but I did not arrive at my journey's end till noon, and by that time the sun had great power. Although it was the middle of the cold season, being January 20th, yet in these Southern plains the heat is always great, as Tinnevelly is only nine degrees from the Equator. The platforms on the line were crowded with dark-faced crowds of natives, whose heads were shaved as far as the top of the crown, but their hair was allowed to grow in a long rough mane behind. Sometimes it was tied up in a knot, and covered with a turban, but more often it hung down their backs in an untidy fashion. I was very hungry before I arrived at my destination, as I had neglected to carry a luncheon basket, and refreshment rooms were noticeable by their absence. However, I brought some plantains, and bread, and obtained a draught of the "milk" of the green cocoa-nut. This is a most delicious beverage. The vendor cuts off the top of the nut with a sharp sickle-shaped knife, and then pours the liquor into your glass. It is nearly white in colour, almost clear, and not in the least like milk. Its taste is sweet, and a drink of it is most refreshing. When the nut ripens this liquor becomes more like milk, but when the nut is in a green state the juice is far nicer to drink.

I arrived at Tinnevelly Station about noon, and drove from there to Palamcottah, about two miles distant. This was my first experience of a "bandy" or bullock waggon, which is the common conveyance of Southern India. The horse "gharri" of the North gives way to the bullock "bandy," and everyone hires it for long journeys. The "bandy" is a two-wheeled waggon, about six feet long and three feet wide. It is entered from the back, and the seats can be so arranged as to form a bed. There is a tilt or covering over the top, made of plaited palm leaves, and the driver sits it front. Good bullocks will trot about six miles an hour, but the hack "bandy" does not travel so fast. Indeed on the sandy tracks away from the towns, two miles an hour is the average pace.

My "bandy" soon brought me to the Church Missionary College at Palamcottah, where I was most kindly received, and arrangements were made for my further journey into the country district. I had been advised to go to the Christian village of Nazareth, which is twenty-one miles distant from Palamcottah. The only means of reaching this village is by "bandy." During the heat of the day I stopped at Palamcottah, and saw a little of the work going on there. The town is the head-quarters of the Church Missionary Society's Mission; it is here that Bishop Sargent resides, and here is also a Training College for native catechists and teachers, with a practising school attached. The buildings were plain and substantial, and seemed well fitted for their purpose. The Rev. T. Kember, who is in charge of this college, was most willing to show me everything, and to explain his plans for the spiritual, mental and physical training of the students. The dormitories were built in native fashion, the students slept on mats spread on the floor, and in no way were they over-Europeanized. They were encouraged to play games, and go in for athletics; the lecture rooms were large, clean, cool, and well fitted with all kinds of apparatus; and the course of study seemed everything that could be desired. There is no work which tends more to the edifying of the native Church than this work of training native agents. If India is ever to be entirely evangelized, it must be through her own countrymen. A large supply of native teachers is absolutely necessary to the growth of the Church. It is good economy to spend much time, and pains, and money, on training picked specimens of the race, who will afterwards be able to teach others. The Missions in Tinnevelly have always been pre-eminent in this branch of the work, and the agents that have been trained in these schools and colleges are now forming the resident clergy and schoolmasters in many Christian villages. The higher the standard held up to the natives who are under instruction, the more will they edify their congregations when they become teachers of others. No pains are too great to be bestowed on those who are to be sent forth, often alone, to bear witness for Christ amongst their heathen neighbours. They have to be taught to be courageous, consistent, pure-minded Christians, not afraid of responsibility, and yet not arrogant and presumptuous. There is need of much wisdom and watchfulness amongst those who try to train the future clergy of India, and on the whole the success has been great. Failures there must be at times. Some fall away from the promise of their youth. But on the whole there is much reason to thank God, and take courage. Those who are sent out from the Training Colleges do hold up a high standard, and often shine like lights amongst those with whom they live.

There seemed to be no jealousy between the missionaries of the Church Missionary Society and those of the Society for the Propagation of the Gospel in Tinnevelly. I certainly was most kindly welcomed by the agents of both Societies. Everyone seemed glad to receive a parson from England, and they all did their best to make my stay pleasant and instructive. I was passed on from one to the other, arrangements were made by which I was to see as much as possible in the short time at my disposal, and there was an amount of kindness shown to me which I can never forget nor in any way repay.

At 4 p.m., when the sun was less powerful, I started in my "bandy" for a drive of twenty-one miles to

Nazareth. For the first part of the way there was a good road, which enabled us to make fair progress. The bullocks trotted along at about five miles an hour, and I was not jolted as much as I expected. But soon we had to turn off the main road, and then our progress was not so rapid. The bullocks required many objurgations to induce them to break into a trot at all, and for the latter part of the journey we had to be content to proceed at a walking pace. The sun had long set, and the road seemed endless. The track seemed to get fuller and fuller of ruts, and I was jolted unmercifully. However, about 9 p.m., we saw the lights of a bungalow. The bullocks quickened up into a last attempt at a trot, there were shouts and cries of welcome, and we drew up at the door of a long, low house with a broad verandah, which seemed crowded with kindly faces. My host and his companion had everything ready for me, and after supper I was ready to ask questions and to hear as much as possible about Mission work.

My first experience of Nazareth was quaint enough. Strangers are so seldom seen in these country villages, that the news of my advent had created quite a stir. If I had been an important Church dignitary, instead of a poor country parson, I could not have caused more excitement. These simple villagers look upon England as such a far off and marvellous land, that they feel complimented by a visit paid to them by any European. They thus are ready to pay honour to anyone who comes to them from abroad, however unimportant his real position may be. I found that the choir boys wished to show me a native dance, that the native clergy had heard of my coming and wished to see me, and that I was expected to preach on the morrow, which was Sunday, to the native congregation. The estimate that they had formed of one unknown and insignificant personage shows how gladly they would receive visits from better known and more illustrious people. I mention this over-appreciation of myself in Nazareth in order that others may visit this interesting village, where they are sure to receive a hearty welcome.

The choir boys duly appeared, late though it was, and we sat out in the verandah to watch the performance. The full glory of a cloudless Indian night was over our heads, and the moon lit up the groups of palm trees and the roofs of the houses round the compound. The dance was founded on an old heathen performance, which had been purified and retained by their Christian teachers. Each boy was dressed in a long white robe like a petticoat, while the upper part of his body was bare. Round his head was a large white turban, and in his hand he carried a circular fan made of the inner wood of the palmyra palm. The performance consisted of swaying the body, changing places, stamping feet, and opening, and shutting, and using the punkahs they carried. During the whole time that these movements went on a song was sung, which was taken up by one and another, and joined in by the whole company. Also some of the dancers held short sticks in their hands, which they struck together, and so marked the time of the dance. Their movements were rapid and graceful; the flowing robes, and swaying figures, and interchanged places, and rhythmical chant combined to make a quaint but pleasing performance. Their alterations of posture and position were all done according to rule, the figures seemed complicated, but the combinations they formed were always effective. I was told that the words of the song were extemporized according to the occasion. Often Bible stories, such as lives of patriarchs, were thus recited. I believe the song I heard was partly in my honour, thanking me for having come so far to see them, but my ignorance of the language prevented me understanding the compliments which were thus paid me.

Nazareth is a village standing in the midst of a district, comprising 48 square miles. In this district there are 46 separate congregations, 39 schools, and nearly 5000 Christians. The staff of clergymen consists of one Englishman and four natives, two of the native clergy being deacons, and two in full orders. In the village of Nazareth there dwell about 1200 people, the majority of whom are palmyra-tree cultivators and small farmers. The Church is a plain oblong structure, capable of holding about 1000 people, when closely packed. As in all native Churches it is not entirely provided with seats, as the bulk of the people prefer to sit on mats spread on the floor. On Sunday there are always five services. Holy Communion at 7 a.m. Mattins and sermon at 9.30 a.m. Litany at 1 p.m. Evensong and sermon at 4 p.m., and again at 7 p.m. The last service is the only one given in English; all the rest are in Tamil. It will thus be seen that Sunday is a busy day for the missionary at Nazareth.

The Sunday that I was there was no special Festival, and the numbers present at the services may be taken as a fair average. Indeed there is a custom, general throughout India, of keeping a written record of the numbers present at every service. The clerk or verger counts the congregation, and the numbers are entered in a book kept for that purpose. Thus any great increase or marked falling off is at once detected, and I was able to tell by the back records that what I saw was no exceptional attendance. At the early Celebration at 7 a.m. there were about 120 communicants. The total number of communicants in the district is 1264, more than one quarter of the total Christian population. It will thus be seen that the proportion of communicants is much larger in Tinnevelly than in England, and that the average attendance is greater than it would be in an English village of the same size. The next service of the day was at 9.30. The choir was surpliced, and marched in procession from the house to the Church. The congregation was very large, the men dressed in white, sitting on one side, while the women draped in bright coloured cloths sat on the other. Out of this large congregation of about 800 people there were only three of us who were English; the rest were all natives. The service was hearty and bright, the singing was well done, and the Tamil lyrics and hymns set to native tunes were evidently popular. I preached through an interpreter; one of the native deacons stood by me, and translated my sermon, sentence by sentence, as it was delivered. It was similar to what I had tried to do at Rangoon,* and I found it equally difficult. The quietness and attention of the congregation were very noticeable; they seemed absolutely motionless. I. did not attend the 1 o'clock Litany, nor the 4 o'clock Evensong, as both of these services were in Tamil. But I went to the 7 o'clock English service, which I had been asked to take throughout. It may sound curious to hear of an entirely English service in an Indian village, but it was originally started by the missionaries for their own satisfaction. They felt it to be refreshing to hear the well-known prayers in their own tongue in a foreign land, and the very sound of the words brought up memories of Sundays spent in the old home across the seas. But now this English service is attended by many native Christians. At Nazareth there are a number of school teachers and catechists who know English, and even some of the schoolboys can follow an English service. So the Church has always a sprinkling of people in it, who join in this (to them) foreign service.

One of the most pleasing features in these evening services is the breaking up of the congregation. They do not disperse quietly as English people do. But they go home in bands and companies singing in chorus one of their favourite lyrics. Nothing could have sounded prettier than these plaintive strains, dying gradually away in the distance, as the people

* See page 130.

departed to their own homes. The moon was up and shed a bright light over the compound. The night was still and quiet. And under the evening stars these strains in an unknown tongue addressed to the true God brought this strange Sunday in a foreign land to a peaceful close.

On the next day I saw as much as I could of the ordinary life and work of a missionary in Nazareth. This village can be taken as a specimen of many others, and what I saw and heard in this one place is a sample of what goes on all through Tinnevelly. The rule in all Christian villages is to hold a daily service in the Church at 7 a.m. and 7 p.m. At Nazareth this is no mere perfunctory performance at which but few attend, but there is an average congregation of about 150 people, who come as a regular thing to begin and end the day with common prayer. They do it of free will and are under no compulsion. They have nothing to gain or get by this outward show of piety. The missionary is poor, and has no large funds to distribute or give away. But it seems to be their custom from a real desire to make their religion a part of their daily life.

This is true about all their doings. Everything is begun and ended with prayer. For instance on the Monday I was there, the missionary was twice asked to come and offer prayer, first at the commencement of the building of a new house, and next at the beginning of some marriage festivities, which were expected to last several days. Both of these requests were made very simply; there seemed to be no superstitious desire to propitiate an angry Deity, but just a desire to have God's blessing on the work in which they were about to engage.

Nazareth is of course specially favoured in having always had a hard working English priest resident in it. The former missionaries have been well known men, and the present clergyman (the Rev. A. Margöschis) does not spare himself. He has been at Nazareth for the last ten years, and is well known by all. He was specially busy during the famine, when numbers of the starving natives were relieved at this village, and there is a large Orphanage now there, which was opened at that time to accommodate the numbers of little children, who were found almost dead by the roadside. These children are now cared for, and educated, and clothed by Christian charity. The orphan boys are taught carpentering, tailoring, and weaving, and the orphan girls learn to make lace. Several of the latter have been married to respectable Christian natives. The care of these Orphanages takes up much of Mr. Margöschis' time. He acts as a father to the whole number of children, and his verandah generally contained one or two little toddlers, who wished to attract his attention and to rummage his pockets for sugar-plums. These small dark babies were very shy at first, but they now look upon him as their best friend.

Besides the Orphanages there are altogether 39 Schools in Nazareth and the district, and they have 1453 children on the rolls. There are Boarding Schools for both boys and girls, where many of the children of the richer Christian natives come to be educated. There is also a Middle School, where the scholars are prepared for the Teachers' Certificate Examination, and from this School come most of the village schoolmasters and mistresses of the district, and there are Elementary Schools, which are open to all who like to come. All these Schools are under Government inspection, and whilst I was there, the Inspector was holding his annual examination. As far as I could judge, the children seemed to be doing well. In the previous year the total grants earned amounted to 4384 rupees, which shows the prosperous condition of the Schools.

The Government Inspector was a native, and a heathen, but he asked to be allowed to attend the evening service in the Church. He only wished to come out of curiosity, but of course he was permitted to enter. There is I believe always a place near the door of native Churches set apart for enquirers.

The Nazareth Day Schools are open to children of any religion. Many of the lads and young men who have come under Christian influence in the Schools are almost persuaded to become converts, but the knowledge that their own family would excommunicate them, and leave them to starve, deters many from taking the final step. In India it requires great moral courage to confess Christ before men.

One of the most interesting sights at Nazareth is the Hospital and Dispensary. Here all suffering natives are welcome, and they come from long distances to ask for advice and medicine. Mr. Margöschis went through a course at St. George's Hospital, and is a very capable doctor and surgeon. For two hours every day he attends at the Hospital and prescribes for his patients. A fee of one anna (about one penny) is all that is charged, and this fee obtains for each person a course of medicine and advice, as long as it is necessary. On an average over one hundred people are attended to every day. This large number of patients shows how greatly this Hospital is valued. Nothing is more likely to attract heathens to Christianity than this unwearying charity.

More direct Evangelistic work is also carried on in this district. Every Tuesday some of the Mission Agents go in small bands to the neighbouring towns and villages, and explain the simple truths of the Gospel. A company of three or four men singing native lyrics soon attracts a crowd, and when the people are assembled, there is an opportunity of speaking to them. The agents are strictly ordered not to speak of the Hindu gods in a needlessly offensive way. To do so would only defeat the very object in view.

I had a pleasant evening walk through the village, and heard something of the daily life of the people.

The houses are built of brick and mud, thatched with the leaves of the palmyra palm. This palm forms the chief wealth of the district. It flourishes in deep sand, where nothing else will grow, and supplies the people with nearly everything they require. The timber is used for rafters and beams, the leaves for thatch, the leaf-stalks for fencing and fuel, and the fruit is edible. But the sweet sap, which exudes from the base of the leaves, is the most valuable of its productions. This begins to flow at the latter end of January, and continues to do so until July. All through these months the palmyra climber is very busy, as his work is to climb the trees and collect the sap. He first has to cut a gash in the branch, and then tie a small earthen pot under the leaves, to receive the sap. This he collects and takes home morning and evening, often having to climb forty trees a day. The labour is great, but the yield is large, and the produce valuable. The sap crystallizes into hard lumps, and is sweet, wholesome, and fattening. Children thrive well upon it, and it makes their little bodies shine. Much is exported as a coarse sort of sugar, which can be refined and converted into a marketable article. If the juice is allowed to ferment, it becomes intoxicating, and is then called toddy.

One of the villagers ascended a palm tree to show me the way in which these trees are climbed. The trunk was perfectly smooth, and the crown of leaves on the top was about fifty feet from the ground. The man tied his ankles together with a strip of cotton, which allowed them to remain about four inches apart. He then grasped the trunk with his arms, clasped his hands together, and holding firmly on to the bark of the tree with the soles of his feet, he lifted himself upwards. By drawing his feet up towards his hands, he was able to reach still higher, and thus by successive "lifts" he ascended the smooth trunk with ease. It reminded me of the motion of a wooden monkey on a stick which we used to purchase at fairs as a childish toy.

Most of the village people are poor, and live chiefly on rice. The land is sandy, but if well irrigated, it will grow anything. All along the banks of the river the paddy fields are numerous, but away from the water there is nothing but deep sand, on which the palmyra palm alone grows.

While the men are busy in the rice fields or collecting the sap from the palms, the women do the work of the house, beat out the rice from the husk, cook the meals, and draw water from the wells. The children are sent to school, and when they come home they are employed in gathering sticks and brush-wood for the fire.

No one who has ever visited such a village as Nazareth can afterwards sneer at the life and work of a missionary. The loneliness and isolation of such a life must be seen to be appreciated. The want of friends like-minded with himself, the constant intercourse with no one but foreigners, the rarity with which any other Englishman is seen, these are necessary hardships of his lot. Besides this solitariness, there is the exhausting climate, the danger of fever, often the unhealthiness of the spot in which his life has to be lived. And on him is laid "the care of all the Churches." He has to be ready with advice, reproof, and mediation. He is the universal referee; the doctor, school-manager, and governor of his little community. The fact of his being an Englishman gives his opinion weight with all, and his house has to be open at all times to his dark-skinned neighbours. His time is taken up with a multiplicity of duties. His patients at the Dispensary, his children at the Schools, the catechists and agents whom he is training, the sick, the sorrowful, the dying, all look for his coming and pour out their troubles into his ear. He has to be the dispenser of such little charity as he is entrusted with, to be in constant want of funds, and yet to make his Schools as efficient as possible. It needs good business habits as well as complete self-denial, and an unwearying faith in the possibilities of human nature being transformed and sanctified by God's Spirit, to make a true missionary. It is so easy to get depressed and downcast. The Source of true strength needs to be sought, or the man becomes irritable and hopeless, and then his work languishes and fails.

I may add here a few facts and figures about Indian Missions taken from Sir Richard Temple's *Oriental Experiences*.* So many people repeat without thought the vulgar objections to the work of missionaries, that the testimony of an unbiassed witness, who had exceptional opportunities for judging, may be useful for the purpose of clearing away some common misconceptions.

He first answers the objection that there is no success obtained by missionaries. Sir R. Temple points out that already there are 390,000 native Christians in India connected with the Church of England, that 100,000 of these are communicants, that there are 300 native clergy, 85 training schools, and 4 normal institutions from which 3000 students are turned out annually. The Schools contain 200,000 children, not all of whom are Christians, and there are 24 mission printing presses, from which three-quarters of a million of religious books issue annually. All these figures show some result already attained. And this distinguished civilian shows further that the number of native Christians has advanced at the rate of 50 per cent. in each decade during the last thirty years. In 1850 the numbers were 92,000; in 1860, 138,000; in 1870, 230,000; in 1880, 390,000. If the same rate continues during the next thirty years, in 1910 there ought to be two million native Christians connected with our Church. These figures are I think worth pondering.

He also meets a further objection that missionaries

* See pp. 132, 136, 137, 140, 141.

lead easy lives, and are idle, lazy, and luxurious. He points out that there are but 500 European missionaries in 493 mission stations. This gives one missionary to every 400 scholars, supposing that they were all employed in education. But besides their work in their Schools and their ordinary parochial ministrations, there is the arduous labour of evangelization and the difficult work of translating the Bible and other books into 20 vernacular languages. Certainly my own experience of missionaries gave me a remarkable idea of the self-denying and continual labour demanded from every one of them. The hardest worked London curate has an easy life compared with that lived by an earnest missionary, who is overwhelmed with the variety and amount of his work, at which he often labours single-handed and with an overpowering sense of all that he has to leave undone.

Further, Sir R. Temple speaks of the cost of converting the heathen, at which many sneers are levelled. He shows that the total cost of the English Church Missions in India is about £400,000, while there are about 400,000 native Christians, and 200,000 scholars, making a total of about 600,000 people under Christian influences. The cost therefore is less than 15 shillings a head per annum; and he does not see how the same amount of work could be done more cheaply

He also answers the objection that natives become Christians for the sake of what they can get. He shows that there are but 4500 natives in the service of the missions, and the male converts may be taken as numbering 200,000. Thus out of every 45 native Christians, only one is in service under the missionaries. This then constitutes no great temptation to entice natives to embrace Christianity. That natives become Christians for the sake of gaining a livelihood thereby sounds ridiculous to those who have seen the poverty of the Mission Stations, and the numbers of Christians gathered together in them. If the missionaries were expected to support all their converts, they and their native *protégés* would have been starved long ago. There may have been once some truth in the old sneer of "rice Christians," that being the name given to those who hoped to get something by their change of religion. But the numbers have now so largely increased that it would be impossible for any missionary to support his flock. As far as I could judge, they were most careful not to pauperize tho people by giving them doles, or teaching them to depend on the gifts of Europeans. They were taught useful trades, such as printing, carpentering, or tailoring, and were encouraged to earn their own living. Sometimes a new convert, who is excommunicated by his family and made an outcast, has for a short time to be helped by charity. But he is soon put in the way of earning his own living, and the Christians in Southern India are now so numerous, that they can afford to laugh at the fear of starvation, which was at one time a threat employed by the relations of those who were inclined to become Christians. Indeed instead of the missionary supporting his flock by charitable doles, the opposite is rapidly becoming the case. The native Church is becoming almost self-supporting, and in many instances the congregation provides entirely for the stipend of its native pastor. Where there is a European clergyman with a higher salary, the poor natives cannot entirely provide his stipend, but even then they give as they are able, and the Societies' funds at home are to that extent saved, and set free to be employed in other districts where the number of Christians are fewer. As much as £20,000 is subscribed annually from native Christians: this shows that instead of being pauperized by doles, they are receiving in most instances nothing themselves, and are learning to pay in many places a large proportion of the salaries of their clergy. Thus there is springing up a feeling of healthy independence, which is wisely fostered by all missionaries.

The common remark that native Christians are

worse than native heathens, that they drink, and lie, and steal, is also I believe a vulgar error. Sometimes it arises from a solitary instance of misbehaviour, which is then taken as typical of the whole community. More often it is a prejudice, which rests on no foundation in fact. The native Christians seemed, as far as I could hear, to be as honest, and faithful, and sober, as Christians at home. They would not compare unfavourably with English villagers, who have been brought up for generations in the faith of Christ. They certainly are far ahead of their heathen neighbours in purity, honesty, peacefulness, and truth. This is now allowed by magistrates and others, who have means of comparison. I think this is the more surprising when we remember how Christ's religion has been sometimes exhibited to the natives of India. The lives of some professing Christians are a disgrace, but too often these Christians are English people, and not natives of India.

From Nazareth I travelled on by "bandy" to another village called Mudalûr. The road was a mere track in the sand, the distance was about ten miles, and the bullocks took five hours to complete the journey. I travelled by night, and so slept most of the way. The bottom of my "bandy" was filled with straw, on which a mattress was spread, and I was able thus to lie at full length, and rest as I journeyed. Mudalûr was the first Christian village founded in Tinnevelly, being a place of refuge in 1797 for a few Christians, who fled thither to escape the persecutions of their heathen neighbours. It then only numbered about 20 people. It now has a population of 1200. It is the centre of a large district 15 miles in circumference, containing 23 villages, of which 19 have Christian congregations. In this district there live some 8000 people, of whom more than 6000 are heathen, and here there lives and works one English missionary, the Rev. H. B. Norman.

Unfortunately in 1877 the Church at Mudalûr fell

down, having been built on insecure foundations, and being exposed to very heavy floods. So the only place for holding service when I was there was the School-room, which barely holds 150 people, and is utterly inadequate to the wants of the village. When I arrived, Mr. Norman was absent at an out-station, but the native clergyman asked me to give a short address at the morning service. He seemed to think the people would like to hear a strange preacher, so I spoke as well as I could to those who were present. I mention this to show what interest the people in Tinnevelly take in visitors. They are very fond of hearing sermons, and any strange clergyman is expected to address them. They were mostly poor village people, scraping a small living from a sandy soil, and very likely oppressed by money lenders. Their clothes were few and poor, and their faces looked thin and careworn, but they came gladly to hear what I could say, and one hoped that they would get some comfort into their hard lives from the good news of the Gospel.

Every effort was being made to build a new Church at Mudalûr, and I saw the beginning of a large and spacious structure which is now completed. This Church will hold 2000 people, and will be one of the handsomest buildings in the whole district. Not long before my visit a friend of Missions visited Mudalûr, and attended a moonlight service in the ruins of the old Church. On his return to Madras he sent an account of his visit to the newspapers, in which he said, "Nearly two thousand people assembled for evening prayer and sermon one evening last week, and the eagerness of the people and their devotion was very interesting. I wished that some *who almost disbelieve in missions* could have seen what I saw." Mr. Norman promised me that if I would stay with him for one more day, and would consent to preach to the people of the district, I should see a congregation which would fill the area of the new Church. It would have been a wonderful experience to preach to such a gathering, but I could not spare the time. I mention it to show how willing the Christians in Tinnevelly are to come to Church and to hear sermons. The people of Mudalûr have been most interested in the rebuilding of their Church. Though they are poor, yet they have given over £100 in money, and £50 more in voluntary labour, which shows how ready they are to do all in their power. The estimated cost of the Church was £1000.

From Mudalûr I went on to another village called Mengnanapuram. This is a station which is worked by the Church Missionary Society, and in it there is the largest Church yet built in Tinnevelly. The red spire of this Church, towering above the palm-trees, is a landmark from far, and the effect of it rising up amongst such tropical scenery is curious and interesting. One so seldom sees Christian architecture in India, that a Church spire in that land looks at present incongruous. But some day one hopes that throughout the length and breadth of the land there will be similar Christian symbols.

Though the distance from Mudalûr to Mengnanapuram was but a few miles, yet as the track was over the sandy plain, our progress was very slow, and I arrived dead beat and almost knocked up with the heat. I think the sun had penetrated through the tilt of the "bandy," and had given me a slight stroke. It prevented me seeing as much as I should otherwise have been able to do of Mengnanapuram. This interesting village has been singularly blest in its pastors. The Rev. Mr. Thomas lived here for forty years, and left his mark on the place. His widow and daughter still dwell in the midst of the people whom they have so long cared for, and Mrs. Thomas says that she will never leave the village, in which she has lived so long. Her life has been devoted to missionary work, and her labours have not yet ceased. She manages two large boarding schools for boys and girls, and is the friend and adviser of all the villagers. There is now no English clergyman resident at Mengnanapuram, but the Church is served by native clergy. Mrs. Thomas is looked up to by all as the mother of the village, and she intends to die where she has spent so large a portion of her life. She has seen a whole generation grow up round her, and the head mistress of her school came to her first as a little girl. Her influence for good is inestimable, and her life has been a model of self-sacrifice. She sees but few Europeans, as there are none living in the village, and the place is necessarily difficult of access as there are no roads to it, but only tracks over the sand of the Terai. But here she has laboured for years, and she has her reward in the affection and reverence which are given to her by all. The Church is a beautiful structure, completed in memory of Mr. Thomas, and the architecture in the interior is well seen, as there are no seats or pews to interfere with the *coup d'œil.*

From Mengnanapuram I had another slow drag over the sand back to Nazareth. I had no time to visit any of the other Christian villages, which are all interesting. I had a very kind invitation to go to Edeyengoody, which is where Bishop Caldwell resides, but I was unable to avail myself of it. Anyone interested in Missions might spend many weeks in Tinnevelly, and thus get a better knowledge of the work which is going on. I had only a glimpse of the work, but I saw enough to understand how hopeful was the prospect in this corner of India.

The chief alteration, which I should venture to recommend to those in authority, is the abolition of the double Bishopric. At present Bishop Caldwell has charge over the Mission Stations belonging to the Society for the Propagation of the Gospel, while Bishop Sargent exercises oversight over those belonging to the Church Missionary Society. Each Society pays its own Bishop, and expects his work to be confined to special stations. Thus the country is not divided geographically into dioceses, but each Bishop visits the villages where there are Missionaries belonging to his own Society. Often one Bishop may be within a few miles of another village, and yet not be able to confirm the children there, because they are under the charge of the sister Society. Time is wasted, and power lost by this double-barrelled arrangement. It is as if in every Diocese in England there was a "High Church" Bishop, and a "Low Church" Bishop, and each was to visit the parishes of his own school of thought. Surely the two great Missionary Societies in England might unite together, and provide between them the salary for one Missionary Bishop, who should be a Suffragan to the Bishop of Madras, and have special charge of native congregations. Then he would visit all villages in Tinnevelly, and be also available to go to any place in the Diocese of Madras, where there were native congregations requiring his services. Thus while the Bishop of Madras exercised a general oversight, and specially devoted himself to the English speaking congregations, his Suffragan would take charge of native congregations, and be available for the Confirmation of native Christians. One may hope that when vacancies occur in the present staff of Bishops, some such re-arrangement may be possible, and both expense be saved, and greater mobility and efficiency be attained.

The presence of two Bishops in Tinnevelly has also led to the too sudden withdrawal of English clergymen. The Bishops have felt that their constant supervision enables them to place native pastors in charge of large villages, who act under their continual oversight. This seems to me to be a mistake, for the native clergy are hardly fit to manage parishes alone, and yet the Bishop is often too far away to enable him to help them with advice. It would seem wiser to leave a few English clergy in charge of the larger stations, who should fulfil the duties of *quasi* Rural

Deans. They could have districts containing several villages under their charge, and be always within reach, if any of the native clergy in the neighbourhood desired their counsel or reproof. Thus while the parochial clergy were chiefly native, there might be an English clergyman appointed to each group of villages, from whom advice could be sought in any emergency. His presence would be a support to the native clergy, and his regular inspection would keep them up to the mark.

The whole district of Tinnevelly might well form one Diocese. There is hardly space there for two active Bishops. As it is, the present Bishops seem often to fulfil duties which might be very well discharged by Archdeacons or Rural Deans. No doubt the present race of native clergy are hardly able to manage large congregations without some European supervision. They are often afraid of responsibility and dread to offend the richer members of their flocks. But the many small points, which arise in village life, and which require the advice and mediation of an educated European, need not all be referred to the Bishop. A neighbouring English clergyman would settle the matter equally well.

The double Episcopate and the too sudden withdrawal of English clergymen appear to me the chief dangers, which are likely to retard the success of the Tinnevelly Missions. Otherwise the organization and administration of the native Church seem admirable. Each district possesses a Church Council, consisting of elected and *ex-officio* members, and these District Councils send representatives to a central Provincial Council, which is under the presidency of the Bishop. The native Christians are really learning to be consistent in conduct, and righteous in their lives, and altogether there is no more hopeful field of missionary labour than Tinnevelly.

I had one more evening service at Nazareth and preached once more through an interpreter. Then I had to start for Palamcottah, spending the night in the "bandy," and getting what sleep I could on the road. But before I left Nazareth I received a deputation from the headmen of the village, who came to thank me for having come so far to see them, and for the words I had spoken to them. Their courteous words of gratitude were touching and humbling, and I left them with mutual expressions of goodwill, and earnest promises of continual remembrance, which I for my part have not forgotten.

From Palamcottah I went by train to Tuticorin, which is one of the ports at which the British India coasting steamers touch, and from there I obtained a passage to Colombo. The steamer anchored about two miles from the shore, and a steam launch conveyed me on board. Soon we started for Ceylon, and the coast of India faded from my sight. It was the 25th January, exactly three months since I first landed at Bombay, and during that time I had visited most of the historic cities of India, and had had a glimpse at all three Presidencies and British Burma. I had travelled through the length and breadth of the land, and had gone from Bombay to Rangoon, and from the Himalayas to Cape Comorin. I had seen Hindus, Mohammedans and Buddhists in their several cities, and had visited their different sacred places. I had made all my railway and steamboat connections, I had carried out all my plans, I had not been laid up with illness for a single day, and I had met with an amount of kindness which can never be forgotten. The whole of my tour had been one unmixed pleasure, and as I left the coast of India behind, I could not but feel thankful for the delightful journey which I had made. My time of holiday-making was drawing to a close. I had still ten days to spend in Ceylon, and then I should have to set my face homewards, and hurry back as fast as steam could take me. But I can only hope that some of my readers may be able to follow my footsteps, and derive as much pleasure from a tour in India as I experienced.

CHAPTER XI.

OUR voyage from Tuticorin to Colombo only took 18 hours, and by 8 o'clock in the morning we were anchored off the coast of Ceylon. Although the distance was only 164 miles, yet the change both in scenery and climate was most surprising. Instead of the sandy wastes and far-stretching plains of India we now saw a shore set thick with cocoa-nut palms and green with the luscious vegetation of the tropics. The land was clothed with verdure to the water's edge, and the feathery crowns of the palm-trees were mirrored in the calm waters of the harbour. The heat was somewhat less, but it seemed more oppressive in consequence of the damp that was present in the air. Colombo is blest with a constant even temperature of about 70°, but it is not a pleasant place of residence, as the dampness of the climate renders exercise almost impossible. The slightest exertion puts one in a bath of perspiration, and this makes the place exhausting and enervating to Europeans.

But for the traveller coming from the dry climate of India, the change to Ceylon is pleasant enough. For he does not stay in the hot damp atmosphere of the coast, but hurries inland to the heights in the centre of the island, where his eyes are gladdened with the perfection of tropical foliage, and his nerves braced by a dry, warm and delicious air. As we lay anchored in the harbour of Colombo we could see far off blue peaks rising inland, and we were shown one conically-shaped hill, which was said to be the summit of Adam's Peak.

Colombo is now the most important port in the island, as the P. and O. steamers have given up calling at Point de Galle. The harbour is well protected by an extensive breakwater, and within its shelter there is safe anchorage for hundreds of ships. The town is built along the shores of the bay, and from the sea the houses appear surrounded with palm-trees. The population is 120,000, and the town extends for about four miles along the sea-shore. As soon as our steamer anchored, we were surrounded by small boats and catamarans, anxious to take us on shore, and the scenery looked so tempting that we did not delay, but soon set foot on the island of Ceylon.

The island is a little smaller than Ireland, and has had a varied history. In ancient days there was a strong kingdom in the north of the island, which had wars with varying success with the Malabars of the coast of India. The capital of this kingdom was at Anaradhapura, which was founded about the 5th century B.C., and flourished for about 1500 years. In more modern times Kandy has been the capital of the island, and when the Portuguese came in 1505, they found a strong government ruling in the highlands of the interior, with whom they had frequent encounters. They and their enemies, the Dutch, fought for the possession of the coast line, and at last the Dutch drove out the Portuguese and established themselves at Galle and Colombo. In 1796 the English obtained all the Dutch settlements, and in 1815 they conquered the Kandyan kingdom, and became masters of the whole island.

The inhabitants of Ceylon are chiefly of two races. The Singalese, who are yellowish-brown, pleasant featured, and effeminate in appearance, and the Tamils, who are dark-skinned immigrants from India. The Singalese are Buddhists, while the Tamils still retain their Hindu religion. The Singalese are the merchants, and landowners, and domestic servants of Ceylon, while the Tamils form the coolie or labourer class. Besides these two races there are also the

Moormen of the coast, who are said to be Persian in origin, and are Mohammedan in religion. They are the pedlars and traders of the island, who do most of the retail business, and are very keen and quick-witted in their bargains. Each of these races has its own peculiar dress, and they are all unmistakable in their appearance. The Singalese are the most curious, as the men grow their hair very long, and anoint it plentifully with cocoa-nut oil. They then part it in the middle, and arrange it in a neat plait or knot behind. On the top of all they place a large tortoise-shell comb, and as both sexes wear petticoats, it is at first difficult to distinguish the beardless men from the women. The long hair and comb give a very comical expression to some faces. Porters and policemen, ticket collectors and waiters, all wear the comb as their only head-dress, and even elderly gentlemen with grey whiskers, who have the appearance of well-to-do tradesmen or merchants, stick a comb into their scant locks and put on a petticoat. When this is combined (as it often is) with European coats and trowsers, the effect is decidedly ridiculous to the unaccustomed eye.

The Tamils looked as hard featured and sad as they did in Southern India. They earn higher wages by thus expatriating themselves, but the coolies have but a hard life in every country. They constitute half the population of Ceylon, as the Singalese are not inclined to do hard work, and refuse to act as common labourers.

The Moormen shave their heads and wear a high cap made of fine grass plaited in colours, and their faces have a Jewish cast of feature. They are very keen traders, and take in the unwary traveller and fleece him unmercifully.

I did not stay more than a few hours in the relaxing climate of Colombo, but started as soon as possible for Kandy, which is now the capital of the island. This town is distant about 70 miles from the sea, and is approached by a railway, which some have called "the most beautiful line in the world." At first we passed through flat lands near the coast, which were overgrown with forests of cocoa-nuts, and rank with the vivid green luxuriance of tropical vegetation. Soon we began to ascend the slopes, and as we climbed upwards we saw the country spread out for miles beneath. Then the hills closed in again on us, and we passed through a gorge in the mountains, which was extremely lovely. The setting sun lit up the peaks and forests through which we passed, and the slopes on all sides were clothed with verdure. After we had passed through the gorge, the hills receded, and we ran on to the flat plateau, on which the town of Kandy is built. Our journey occupied four hours, and during that time we ascended 1500 feet.

Kandy lies in a cup amongst the hills, which surround it on all sides. The town is built on the edge of an artificial lake, and the reflections in the water add to the charm and beauty of the place. The Governor has a house in this beautiful spot, and a large number of English reside in or near Kandy. Many of the neighbouring hills have been laid out as coffee plantations, and the houses of the planters are seen far up amongst the trees. All round the town walks have been laid out on the sides of the hills overlooking the lake, and peeps have been opened out through the luxuriant jungle. Overhead tall trees give grateful shade, and on all sides creepers, and flowering shrubs, and thick undergrowth, cover the hills. All sorts of palms flourish and abound; the cocoa-nut with its feathery crown mingles with the tall and graceful areca and palmyra, while the strange fan-shaped tallipot looks quaint and unlovely. Over the houses roses grow in profusion, and the plumbago and the bouganvillier are common creepers. In the hedge-rows the datura clambers, showing everywhere its large white trumpet-shaped flowers. The luxuriance and splendour of the vegetation must strike the most unbotanical traveller.

But the place where the vegetable kingdom is seen at its best, is in the beautiful Peridenyia Gardens. These are kept up by the Government, and are said to be the most beautiful in the world. They are laid out on the side of a river, and are full of all sorts of rare and beautiful trees. Palms, and ferns, and foliage plants flourished abundantly, and on the banks of the river there were clumps of giant bamboos 50 feet high. Luxuriant creepers climbed up to great heights, and were covered with blossoms. The taste shown in the arrangement of the Gardens, combined with the natural beauty of the spot and the perfection of the soil and climate, renders this one of the most lovely places I saw in my travels.

The one shrub which has of late years failed to flourish, and which formerly was the most valuable product of Ceylon, is the coffee plant. Twenty years ago every hill-side in the district above Kandy had its plantation, and there seemed no end to the fortunes which might be made by the cultivation of coffee. Then there was a surplus in the revenues of the Island, and the planters were a successful body of men. But latterly all things have changed, and a blight has settled down over the chief industry of the Island. A mysterious disease has attacked the plant, and square miles of shrubs are seen with scarcely a leaf on their branches. The cause of this disease is said by some to be the exhaustion of the soil from over-production; others attribute it to the excessive manuring of the ground. Certainly the fact is patent enough, whatever may be the cause. A sort of fungus appears on the green leaf and destroys it, as the potato plants are destroyed in England. The coffee shrub itself has the appearance of a laurel, but where the disease attacks the plant, the leaves drop off and the berries do not ripen. Planters are now putting chinchona and cacao plants in their coffee gardens.

Tea is also being cultivated with success, but the days of Ceylon coffee seem to have come to an end.

At Kandy there is one of the most sacred shrines of the Buddhist faith, popularly called the Tooth Temple, which is built on the edge of the artificial lake. The building itself is a long, low structure, not architecturally beautiful. The relic, which gives the name to the temple, is said to be one of the teeth of Gautama Buddha himself. It is seldom shown, but the box in which it is kept is exhibited, adorned with gold and precious stones. There seems great doubt as to the antiquity of the present relic. History relates that the original tooth of Buddha was taken by the Portuguese after their conquest of Kandy. An enormous sum was offered for its ransom, but the Archbishop of Goa would not sanction the encouragement of what he considered to be idolatry. So the request of the Kandyan King and his money were refused, and the tooth was rammed into the mouth of a cannon, and fired out to sea, thus being utterly destroyed. However it has in some way been restored to its original home, and the history of its destruction is forgotten, and the present tooth receives all the reverence which could be shown to the most authentic relic of the great Gautama Buddha. Those who have seen the tooth say that it has no appearance of being a human tooth, but is a piece of bone about two inches long, which looks like the tusk of some animal. However the genuineness of the relic is not doubted by any Singalese Buddhist.

From Kandy I went to Anaradhapura, which was in ancient times the seat of a powerful monarchy and the capital of the Island. The journey was tiring and uncomfortable, but the marvellous ruins I there saw amply repaid me for the difficulty of reaching the spot. I first took the train to Matalé, which is about 15 miles from Kandy, and from there I journeyed by bullock coach 70 miles further. It was the longest ride I ever took, and we were 18 hours doing the distance. The conveyance was a sort of open waggonette, and we changed bullocks about every 10 miles. The animals were small, but trotted along at a fair rate, and the road was excellent. The scenery throughout was most beautiful, our way lying between steep hills covered with the densest forest, and creepers and undergrowth rendered the jungle almost impervious. Here whole herds of wild elephants roam undisturbed, and are absolutely hidden by the thickness of the forest growth. All night we rattled onwards, and I got what sleep I could, disturbed by the objurgations addressed to the bullocks, and the resounding thwacks with which their poor sides were belaboured. By 6 a.m. we arrived at our destination, having left Matalé at noon on the previous day.

Anaradhapura was founded about the 5th century B.C., and was for many centuries the capital of a flourishing kingdom, which waged wars with the neighbouring states on the coast of India. But its chief interest lies in the fact that it is the spot in Ceylon where the most sacred relics of Buddha were placed, or where the oldest dagobas (or pagodas) were erected in his honour. The introduction of Buddhism into Ceylon took place about the year 245 B.C. The preacher of the new faith was Mahinda, the son of the great King Asoka, who reigned near Patna, in Lower Bengal, and it is a proof of the missionary character of the Buddhist religion that it could spread so far, so soon after its foundation. The mission to Ceylon was a great success. The reigning King became a zealous adherent of the new religion, and he built the Thuparama Dagoba, which is still one of the glories of the ruined city of Anaradhapura.* Soon after the building of this dagoba other missionaries came from India to Ceylon, and one of them, the sister of Mahinda, brought with her a branch of the sacred Bo Tree then flourishing at Buddha Gaya,

* See Rhys David's *Buddhism*, p. 230.

which was believed to be the very tree under which Gautama had experienced that mental conflict which is called his attainment of Buddha-hood.* The slip off this sacred tree was planted at Anaradhapura, and took root and grew. It still flourishes, and is now the oldest historical tree in the world. Buddhism continued to increase in Ceylon, and is still the religion of the Singalese nation. Although India has for many centuries deserted the Buddhist faith, yet its missionaries gained converts in other lands, whose descendants still claim Gautama of India as the founder of their religion. Ceylon is like Burma, China, Siam, and Corea. It still clings to that pure rule of life, which took its rise in India, but has been discarded in its native home. For while India has sunk back into idolatry and superstition, and is again bound by the fetters of caste which Gautama broke, Ceylon still holds that purer creed which the missionary labours of Mahinda brought thither in the 3rd century B.C.

Nothing but ruins mark the site of the once flourishing city of Anaradhapura. Indeed until twenty years ago the very ruins were hadly discoverable. Thick jungle had so overgrown the site of this once famous town that the wonders of its remains were entirely unknown. However fortunately Mr. Dickson was appointed some fifteen years ago to be the resident Government Agent at Anaradhapura, and he devoted himself to exploration and was rewarded by many discoveries. The Buddhist monks welcomed him as a friend, and he has had the satisfaction of clearing away the growth of centuries, and bringing again to light many archæological treasures. Roads have been opened out in all directions, and the ruins are now carefully preserved and can be well seen.

The most striking features of this ruined city are the dagobas. These are immense mounds of solid

* See *ante* p. 112.

brickwork, of circular design, raised over some relic. They are now overgrown with trees and shrubs, which have found foothold in the crumbling surface of the masonry. The labour expended on these masses of solid building must have been enormous, and the number of bricks in each of the larger dagobas is greater than that used in the construction of an ordinary English county town. The largest dagoba is 400 feet in diameter and 236 feet high, and there are two others which nearly equal it in mass and height. The outer surface of the structure is now crumbling away, but no time can affect these enormous masses of solid brickwork. They have stood for over 2000 years, and their ruins will continue much as they are now for an indefinite time longer. Whether they contain any treasures is a moot point. To drive a tunnel or adit into one of them, in the hope of discovering a central chamber filled with relics, and perhaps sacred writings on metal plates, would be an experiment that every archæologist would desire to see effected. If carefully performed there would be no danger to the dagoba, and even the monks if wisely handled might make no objection to such an exploration. If anyone could attempt such an interesting investigation it would be Mr. Dickson, who is already well known and trusted by everyone in Ceylon. I wish he would attempt such an exploration, and thus crown the work he has already done for Anaradhapura.

Besides the great dagobas there are numberless other evidences of the former wealth and importance of this ruined city. Everywhere in the jungle one meets with carved and shaped stones. Under the turf are discovered semicircular slabs richly carved with figures of men and animals. There are numerous figures cut in the sides of the stone staircases which lead up to many-pillared halls, which were used as preaching stations. There are bathing ponds made of squared stones arranged in steps, drinking troughs for elephants hollowed out of great blocks of rock, carved pillars in countless profusion, everywhere the remains of a large city which covered an area of many square miles. All these signs of a rich and flourishing civilization are now overgrown by the densest jungle, which needs to be constantly cut back lest it should once more cover up what has been already discovered.

But the most interesting of all the sights of Anaradhapura is the sacred Bo Tree, the oldest historical tree in the world. Planted originally from a slip brought from the parent trunk by a daughter of King Asoka, it still grows and flourishes, while the sacred tree at Buddha Gaya has, I believe, ceased to exist. It is propped and supported by terraces of brick work, which keep it from splitting. Round it there are several younger Bo Trees, and in their branches a colony of monkeys live and play. The sacred tree is always guarded by a Buddhist monk, and such is the veneration attached to it that even a leaf from it may not be plucked. Sir Emerson Tennent compares its age with that of other famous trees. He says,

> Ages varying from one to four thousand years have been assigned to the *Baobabs* of Senegal, the *Eucalyptus* of Tasmania, the *Dragon tree* of Orotava, the *Wellingtonia* of California, and the chestnut of Mount Etna. But all these estimates are matter of conjecture; and such calculations, however ingenious, must be purely inferential: whereas the age of the Bo Tree is *matter of record*, its conservancy has been an object of solicitude to successive dynasties, and the story of its vicissitudes has been preserved in a series of continuous chronicles, among the most authentic that have been handed down by mankind. Compared with it the Oak of Ellerslie is but a sapling, and the Conqueror's Oak in Windsor Forest barely numbers half its years. The Yew Trees of Fountain's Abbey are believed to have flourished there 1200 years ago; the Olives in the garden of Gethsemane were full grown when the Saracens were expelled from Jerusalem; and the Cypress of Sorna, in Lombardy, is said to have been a tree in the time of Julius Cæsar: yet the Bo Tree is older than the oldest of these by a century, and would almost seem to verify the prophecy pronounced when it was planted, that it would flourish and be green for ever.*

The botanical name of the tree is *ficus religiosa*,

* Sir E. Tennent's *Ceylon*, vol. ii., p. 613.

and it is allied to the banyan. It is watered by the monks in seasons of drought, and their constant care has enabled it to live so long.

The ruins of Anaradhapura prove that in ancient times the interior of Ceylon must have been much more thickly populated than it is at present. There seems no reason why the soil should not support many more people than now dwell in the island. What is now thick jungle was once cultivated land, and if the ruined tanks were repaired, and a thorough system of irrigation established, rice and other crops might be profitably raised. The resources of Ceylon have never been fully developed. There are square miles of land overgrown with forest, which might grow crops. But the struggle for existence is not keen, the population is thin, life is easy, and the Singalese take no trouble to increase the productiveness of the country. Coming from India where every patch of fertile soil is so carefully cultivated, the difference between the two countries is very marked.

Probably the easiest way to develop the resources of Ceylon, and to save its revenues, would be to annex it to the Government of India. The present system of government is wasteful and unnecessarily expensive, and there seems no reason why the Island should not be removed from the care of the Colonial Office and be placed under the India Office, with which its geographical position appears naturally to connect it. Then a Chief Commissioner would be sent from India to rule the Island instead of a more highly paid Governor from England, and the whole administration would be in subordination to the Governor at Madras. The Chief Commissionership of Ceylon would then be similar to that of Burma, a post held by a rising civilian who would prove in this *quasi* independent position, whether he was fit for still higher office. The military charges would also be lessened, and the troops in Ceylon would be under the control of the Commander-in-Chief at Madras. Indian civilians have also learnt how to treat subject races, and half the population of the Island consist of Tamil emigrants from India. There seems no question that by thus making Ceylon an *annexe* to Madras, the Island would gain a more efficient yet cheaper government.

At present, however, no such change is likely to be made, for Ceylon is looked upon as one of the prizes of the Colonial Service, and the Governorship is a piece of patronage that the Colonial Secretary would dislike parting with. Still now is the time to ventilate such changes, for Ceylon is suffering from extreme poverty, in consequence of the failure of the coffee plantations, and retrenchment in expenditure is much discussed. Certainly one of the easiest ways of saving money would be this proposed annexation to India.

I came back from Anaradhapura to Kandy by the same route, again having a long ride of 18 hours in the bullock coach. A few days after I returned from Kandy to Colombo, where I was to take the steamer for England. I had no time to see more of Ceylon, and had to give up visiting the interesting district of Newera Ellia, which is the sanatorium of the Island, lying high up amongst the mountains of the interior.

While I was waiting for the steamer at Colombo, I was fortunate enough to be taken over a cocoa-nut oil factory, which is one of the most successful manufactories in the Island. The whole of the low lands of Ceylon are covered with forests of cocoa-nut palms, and these graceful trees form one of the main features of the scenery. The oil is extracted from the inner rind of the nut, and these apparently useless tough envelopes are brought in thousands to the factory by the country people. It takes the rinds of 10,000 nuts to make one cask of oil, and therefore millions of these rinds are used up. They are crushed, and ground, and pressed under hydraulic rams, and the oil is thus squeezed out of them; it is then placed in casks, and sent to the Continent, where it is used in the manufacture of soap. After the oil has been extracted, the refuse of the rinds is made into a sort of cake, and exported to England to be used as food for cattle. The factory is very large, and the sheds and yards cover 12 acres of ground. All the products of Ceylon are here prepared for exportation, and I saw chests of coffee, chinchona, and tea ready for transshipment. Thousands of coolies are employed in the works, and it is one of the most flourishing industries in the Island.

My holiday was now drawing to a close, and on February 7th I left Colombo by a P. and O. steamer. I was very glad to have had this short peep at Ceylon, and I should advise all who make a tour in the East to include it if possible in their route. The scenery is most beautiful, the climate away from the coast is delightful, and the people and buildings are well worth seeing. Its green loveliness, its shore fringed with palms bending over the surf, its hills clothed with forests twined with creepers, its rivers flowing between banks covered with bamboos, its woods bright with many flowering shrubs, its air soft and delicious and heavy with the scent of tropical flowers, its nights spangled with stars and specked with fire-flies, all come back in pleasant memories and make a picture which can never be forgotten. This Island set in the midst of southern seas has a charm of its own, and it is one of the most beautiful possessions of our Colonial Empire.

My voyage homewards must be quickly passed over. We had a calm passage over the Indian Ocean. In eight days we reached Aden, and in five days more we anchored at Suez. There I left the ship, and went by train to Cairo to see a little of the land of Egypt. I was able to spend a week in Cairo, and I saw a few of the ordinary sights. But my time was too short to get more than a glimpse at the country, and I was only there long enough to feel the peculiar fascination which Egypt always exercises on all who visit it. There is a saying that "he who has once drunk the

Nile water ever wants to drink it again," and certainly there is no country which has a stronger attraction for the casual traveller. Even after the beautiful buildings of India, there was much to charm and delight the eye, and the incredible antiquity of the remains enlarged one's historic sense. To gaze on the Pyramids of Gizeh, or to study the sculptures at Sakkhara, and then to realize that these buildings are anterior to the time of Moses, and may even date back to the era of Abraham, gives one a distinct shock, and throws the antiquity of all other buildings into the shade. In the Boulak Museum one is shown the mummied form of the (probable) Pharaoh of the Book of Exodus, together with the richest collection of Egyptian antiquities in the world. If Cairo had shared the fate of Alexandria, and been burnt by Arabi's rebellious army, and if the Boulak Museum had perished, the loss to archæology would have been irreparable.

Cairo was full of troops, the Citadel was held by our forces, and the bare-legged Highlander was a common sight in the bazaars and streets. The driver of my donkey had many tales to tell about the state of the city, when the Khedive was a prisoner at Alexandria, and when Arabi was raising levies to face the English troops at Tel-el-Kebir. My donkey-man said that he had had to flee to Upper Egypt to escape impressment, but his stories had to be taken with a certain amount of caution, as it was probable that he said whatever he thought would please me.

Walks through the Bazaars, visits to the principal Mosques, and a look at one of Ismail's numerous Palaces, filled up the short time at my disposal. The extravagance and wastefulness of the late ruler of Egypt are nowhere more evident, than in these large, over-adorned Palaces, full of expensive French furniture, and gaudily ornamented with gilt mouldings and immense mirrors. While Egypt was ever approaching nearer and nearer to national bankruptcy, and while the poor *fellaheen* were ground down by an intolerable weight of taxation, the late Khedive was wasting the resources of the country in building useless Palaces, and following the worst fashions of the French Imperial Court.

There was much talk everywhere of the future of Egypt. Then were the days when Lord Dufferin had just arrived, and when Hicks Pasha's illfated expedition was starting for the Soudan. Concerning this last event I heard sharp criticism on the ignorancc of some of the European officers, who went forth with no experience of desert warfare. Such officers, although called Captains and Lieutenants, were quite ignorant of the ways of the enemy, and were not likely to be of much use in the time of need. At least they died bravely, and victory was hardly possible. Yet at that time no Egyptian minister was prepared to advise the retrocession of the Soudan, and it required a sharp lesson before the Egyptian Government discovered the rottenness of its military condition.

From Cairo I went by rail to Ismailya, which is the chief town on the Suez Canal, about equidistant from Port Said and Suez. Here I hoped to meet with the steamer, which was to carry me back to England, but I had to endure first a tiresome delay. Two ships had gone aground in the Canal, and the whole traffic of the world was stopped in consequence. Thus I had to spend three days at Ismailya, waiting for my steamer, which could not move until the obstructionists were afloat again.

I do not recommend any traveller to stay at Ismailya if he can possibly help it. It is a town, which has sprung up on the edge of Lake Timsah, and it only exists because here are the headquarters of the Canal traffic. All the movements of vessels are arranged by telegraph from the office at this place, and here it is settled what ships are to be given precedence, and what ships are to tie up to the bank at the passing stations, so as to make room for their more fortunate rivals. There is a model of the Canal in the office, and small flags are moved about it, indicating what is the position of the corresponding vessels. The office is in telegraphic communication with signal stations all along the banks of the Canal, and as the vessels pass along their movements are notified to the head office, which gives instructions concerning them. The model is an interesting sight, but when no change is made in it for three days, the traveller, who is anxious to get on, finds his frequent visits to the office tiresome to the officials and unedifying to himself.

Besides visiting the office of the Canal Company there is but little to do at Ismailya. The town is built between the Desert and the Bitter Lake. There is one hard road out of the town for three miles, leading to a Palace which was erected on the banks of the Canal for the temporary occupation of the Empress of the French, when she came to the opening ceremony. On all other sides of the town the sandy wastes extend for miles. It is probable that some day the head office will be removed to Port Said, and then Ismailya will be of less importance. Its chief title to fame of late years lies in the fact that it formed the base for Lord Wolseley's advance on Cairo in 1882. The lake was then full of transports and ships of War, and the place was full of troops. When I was there, our forces were only represented by a small detachment of soldiers and a gun-boat.

During my enforced stay at Ismailya, I had the pleasure of meeting M. Naville, the Swiss explorer. He had just been excavating some neighbouring ruins at Tel-el-Mahuta, and had had the satisfaction of proving by the inscriptions he discovered that here was the site of Pithom, the "treasure city," or "store city," mentioned in Exodus as built by the enslaved Israelites for the King of Egypt. He had even discovered a great building, unlike any temple or palace, and probably identical with the granary which constituted this place a "treasure city." I wish I had been able to visit the explorations, but it was impossible.

On March 2nd the block in the Canal was at last removed, and my steamer (and 15 others) arrived at Ismailya. On the 7th we touched at Malta, on the 11th we reached Gibraltar, and on the 15th March I landed at Plymouth. We were just in time for the morning express, and so I reached my own parish that evening. It was the very day that I had planned to be at home, when I had started nearly six months before. I had thus kept my time exactly, and the Parson's holiday was over.

In conclusion I would recommend everyone who has the time and money at his disposal to follow my footsteps. Nothing could be more delightful than a holiday spent in this way. Such a tour enables one to visit India at the very best season of the year. The climate is perfect, wet weather is impossible, and the heat is not excessive. The interest of such a trip is most varied; scenery, costumes, buildings, people, all claim attention. The different religions and the various nations with their diverse customs constantly excite one's interest. And in addition to other matters every parson must feel desirous to see something of mission work, and to enquire into the various efforts which are being made to instruct and evangelize the heathen. The native Churches, the Schools, and Colleges, and Mission Stations, all overflow with interest, and the time seems too short and the days too few to see half that one would like to see. I think the reflex action of all this sightseeing on oneself does good. One returns to one's quiet country parish with ideas enlarged and sympathies widened, and with a store of memories and a recollection of unnumbered kindnesses which no time can obliterate nor age deface.

I have shown that it is possible, without overstepping the legal holiday which is permitted to an incumbent, to visit most of the centres of interest in India, and Burma, and Ceylon, and to get at least glimpses of the lives and manners of our fellow-subjects in the East. Others may follow my example, and diverge from my route, and discover fresh points of interest, which I overlooked. But no one will ever meet with more kindness, or enjoy a happier holiday, than I did in the winter of 1882–83.

FINIS.

INDEX.

Administration of India, 81.
Agra, Fort, &c., 54.
Ajmere, 33.
Akbar, 43, 53.
Alexandria, 3.
Ambir, 39.
Anaradhapura, 214.
Architecture, Hindu, 169.
Arhai-din-ka-Jhonpra, 34.

Babus, Educated, 102.
Bandy, 186.
Bangalore, 153.
Baroda, 28.
Benares, 84.
Bishops in Tinnevelly, 205.
Bombay, 4.
Bo Tree, 217.
Brahmo Somaj, 102.
Buddhism, 113.
——— compared with Christianity, 124.
——— in Ceylon, 214.
Burma, History of, 105.
Burmese, 108.

Cairo, 221.
Calcutta, 99, 100.
Caldwell, Bishop, 183, 204.
Calingapatam, 144.
Cambridge Mission, 50.
Camp Service, 73.
Canning College, 78.
Caste Prejudices, 162.
Catechist, Work of, 171.
Cave Temples, 24.
Cawnpore Massacre, 64.
Ceylon, 208–220.
Choultry, 165, 179.
Christians, Native, 152, 185, 198.
Christmas-Day Services, 129.
Civilian, Life of, 83.
Clergy, Native, 155, 206.
Climbing Palm-tree, 196.
Cocoa-nut Factory, 219.
Code, Indian, 16.
Coffee in Ceylon, 212.
Colombo, 208.
Commissioner, 82.
Communicants, Number of, 191.
Cowley Fathers, 14.

Dagoba, 214, 215.
Dance, Native, 190.
Darjeeling, 91–93.
Delhi, 46, 47.
Deserted Bungalow, 160.
Dickson, Mr., 215.
Durbar, Viceroy's, 74.
Durria dowlut, 160.

Educational Problems, 17.
Egypt, 220.
Elephanta Caves, 6.
Elephants at work, 136.
English Church in India, 181.
Eurasians, 35.
Evangelistic work, 175, 195.
Everest, Mt., 97.
Explorers in Tibet, 95.

Famine in S. India, 183.
——— Results of, 184.
Futtehpore Sikri, 58.

Gáekwár, 29.
Ganapati, 9.
Gautama Buddha, History of, 112.
——— ——— Doctrines of, 113
——— ——— Statues of, 116.
Golden Temple, 86.
Gopura, 165.
Government in India, 79.
——— in Ceylon, 219.
——— House, 100.

Hicks Pasha's Expedition, 222.
High Schools, 19, 172.
Himalayas, 96.
Hinduism, Modern, 90.
H'tee, 116, 141.

Hyder Ali, 156.

Ideas of Empire, 61.
Ignatius, Rev. Mr., 154.
Illumination of Ghâts, 85.
Imambara, 69.
Ismailya, 222.
Itmad-ud-Dowlah, 56.

Jain Temple, 34.
Jehanghir, 43.
Jeypore, 36.
Jumma Musjid, 47.

Kandy, 211.
Karli Cave, 23.
Kember, Rev. T., 187.
Kinchingunga, 96.
Kincob, 89.
Kioung, 119.
Kutub Minar, 49.

Lamaism, 94.
Lawrence, Henry, 72.
Lepers' Hospital, 10.
Lhassa, 94.
Linga, 7.
Locusts, 23.
Lucknow, 69, 70.

Madras, 149, 150.
Madura, 178.
Mantapa, 165.
Margöschis, Rev. A., 193–195.
Marhattás, 8.
Marks, Rev. Dr., 127.
Martinière College, 76.
Masula Boats, 144.
Mayo College, 32.
Memorial Church, 65.
Mengnanapuram, 203.
Merit, Doctrine of, 114, 116, 118, 122.
Missionary Statistics, 185, 199.
——— Methods of, 11, 13.
——— Objections to, 197.
Missionaries, 127, 171, 177, 185, 189, 197.
Moguls, Empire of, 43.
Mohammedans, 45.
Monasteries, 119.
Monkey Temple, 87.
Moormen, 210.
Mosque, Arrangement of, 48.
Moti Musjid, 55.
Moulmein, 134.
Mudalûr, 201.
Mutiny, 63, 66.
Mysore, 156.

Nana Sahib, 63.
Native States, 41.
Naville, M., 223.
Nazareth, 189, 191, 195.
Nga-pee, 134.
Nirvana, 113.
Norman, Rev. H. B., 201.

Officer, District, 82.
Orphanage at Nazareth, 194.
Oudh, History of, 68, 69.
Oxford Mission, 101.
Pagodas, Use of, 114.
Palace, Maharajah's, 37, 166.
Palamcottah, 187.
Palms, 196, 211.
Parvathi, Temple of, 10.
Pegu, 139.
Peridenyia Gardens, 212.
Pithom, Discovery of, 223.
Pohngyees, 122.
Poona, 8.
Prayer Wheels, 98.
Preaching through Interpreter, 130, 192.
Princes, Native, 167.
Prome, 131.

Railway Travelling, 25.
Rajputs, 30.
Rangoon, 107.
Resident, Duties of, 28.
"Rice Christians," 200.
Rice Trade, 110.

Salt Tax, 145.
Sargent, Bishop, 183, 187.
Schools, 16, 172, 174, 194.
School of Art, 153.
Schwartz, 166.
Sekundra, 60.
Seringapatam, 159.
Services at Nazareth, 191, 193.
Shah Jehan, 43.
Shoe Question, 75.
Shway Dagohn, 114.
Singalese, 209.
Srirangham, Temple of, 169.
St. Stephen's College, 52.
Suez Canal, 223.

Taj Mahal, 56.
Talukdars, 78.
Tamils, 151, 175, 192, 209.
Tanjore, 164.
Tea Plantations, 93.
Temple, Sir R., on Missions, 198, 199.
Temple, Arrangements of, 164, 170.
Tents, 27.
Thomas, Rev. Mr. and Mrs., 203.
Tibet, 94.

Timber Yards, 136.
Tinnevelly, 182, 186–207.
Tipu Sahib, 157, 159, 160.
Tooth Temple, 213.
Towers of Silence, 5.
Training College, at Palamcottah, 187.
Trichinopoly, 168–178.
Trimul Naik, 179.
Tuticorin, 207.

Viceroy's Camp, 72.
Victoria School, Poona, 18.
Village Life at Nazareth, 196.
Vimana, 164.
Vishnu, 164.
Vizagapatam, 145.

Well at Cawnpore, 66.
Wrestling, 20.
Wyatt, Rev. J. L., 171.

Zodiacal Light, 144.